D0841904

MEDICO-LEGAL ESSENTIALS

Consent to Treatment

MEDICO-LEGAL ESSENTIALS

Consent to Treatment

JANE LYNCH

LLB (Hons), Legal Dip, Solicitor, FRSM

Forewords by

LOUISE M TERRY

Senior Lecturer in Law and Ethics
Faculty of Health and Social Care
London South Bank University

SUE BATTERSBY

Independent Midwifery Researcher/Lecturer

and

COLUM J SMITH

LLB, Solicitor
Partner, McMillan-Williams Solicitors

Radcliffe Publishing
Oxford • New York

Radcliffe Publishing Ltd
18 Marcham Road
Abingdon
Oxon OX14 1AA
United Kingdom

www.radcliffepublishing.com

Electronic catalogue and worldwide online ordering facility.

© 2011 Jane Lynch

Jane Lynch has asserted her right under the Copyright, Designs and Patents Act 1998 to be identified as the author of this work.

All rights reserved. No part of this publication may be reproduced, stored in a retrieval system or transmitted, in any form or by any means, electronic, mechanical, photocopying, recording or otherwise, without the prior permission of the copyright owner.

British Library Cataloguing in Publication Data

A catalogue record for this book is available from the British Library.

ISBN 13: 978 184619 224 1

Typeset by Pindar NZ, Auckland, New Zealand
Printed and bound by Cadmus Communications, USA

Contents

Foreword

This will be a very useful book for healthcare professionals of all kinds to refer to for a simple-to-understand overview of the law of consent to treatment. The structure is, for the most part, well thought out so topics flow. There are useful checklists for children and human tissue. Chapters include examples and sometimes tasks/activities. These are helpful devices for concentrating students' thinking and enabling them to engage with the subject.

Dr Louise M Terry
Senior Lecturer in Law and Ethics
Faculty of Health and Social Care
London South Bank University
August 2010

Foreword

Consent to treatment is a complex issue fraught with pitfalls for the unwary health professional. This book works through the issues in a straightforward and unambiguous manner that will enhance the knowledge and understanding of all those who read it. It clarifies the legal requirements in relation to consent for treatment but does so with the minimal use of legal jargon making it easy to read and comprehend.

The book contains tasks for the reader to undertake as well as case reviews to facilitate understanding. The examples are taken from a range of scenarios applicable to a wide diversity of healthcare domains. It would be an excellent core text on many health professionals' basic and post-basic courses especially doctors, nurses, midwives and health visitors. The content of the book is also applicable to many associated professions, e.g. physiotherapists, ambulance personnel and care workers.

The checklists are practical work tools which could assist in developing and enhancing good practice. This book is invaluable to healthcare professionals and could help prevent them from attending court defending the care they have inadvertently provided.

Dr Sue Battersby
Independent Midwifery Researcher/Lecturer
August 2010

Foreword

This book explains the complexities of consent in a practical and straight-forward way making a difficult and often complex subject easy to understand. In addition it is a useful handbook that health professionals at all levels can refer to as an everyday text to help guide them through the intricacies of the topic. Consent is an area of clinical practice that clearly over laps with the law on a daily basis. Decisions made in relation to consent have far reaching implications for both patients and health professionals particularly where consent intermingles with, as is often the case, a lack of clear documentation. The law can be easily misunderstood and misapplied by health professionals unless they ensure that they are fully familiar with the relevant provisions. This book is a good starting point. There is a clear use of practical examples and scenarios to consider which allows the reader to reflect on the issues. It promotes safe patient care. With the recent changes in legislation affecting consent this book is an essential tool for all health professionals.

Colum J Smith
LLB, Solicitor
Partner, McMillan-Williams Solicitors
August 2010

Preface

The law relating to consent over the past few years has changed and has become an everyday concern to health professionals. The health professional has an obligation to obtain consent of the patient before they can treat them. If they fail to comply with the law of consent the patient may bring a civil claim for compensation. The health professional is also in danger of committing a criminal offence. The health professional will be accountable for their actions and the complexities of consent leaves them vulnerable.

I have often heard it said 'well if the patient came into hospital that is implied consent to be treated', 'unless the patient refuses treatment in writing then they are consenting to treatment', 'the patient had dementia and therefore lacked capacity to give consent', 'the patient was unconscious therefore I can treat them' – the law does not uphold these views, an unconscious patient implies nothing.

A signature on a consent form does not in itself constitute valid consent. There are a lot of other considerations that must be taken into account such as – how old are they, did they have capacity, how much information did the health professional give them and did they understand it. Asking someone else, such as a family member, to sign a consent form does not constitute valid consent.

The law of consent is not simple to interpret and apply so it is hardly surprising that consent is often inadvertently misunderstood or misapplied by health professionals.

Legal claims relating to consent issues are increasing. Often claims arise because of a lack of understanding by the health professionals of the law and principles relating to consent. Sadly, many claims are also brought because there is no evidence from the records that valid consent was obtained, notwithstanding consent may actually have been validly obtained. Standard consent forms are often not explicit enough. A good standard of record keeping will avoid this situation but the health professional must be fully conversant with the issues of consent in order to make an appropriate entry in the records.

Health professionals are often left floundering when faced with a patient in difficult situations such as a pregnant mother who refuses a caesarean section when the unborn child is in distress, a patient who has a learning disability or someone intent on self-harm. This book seeks to explain the issues of consent as it applies in England and Wales in a simple and straight-forward way, setting out the professional obligations, the basic principles of consent and then the details, which can then be applied to all situations. This will enable the health professional to approach consent in practice in a methodical way to ensure that consent is validly obtained. The aim of the book is to enhance good practice and good patient care.

The examples used are drawn from situations faced by health professionals and real cases. The basic principles should be taken and applied to the health professionals' own situations. Throughout the book many questions will be posed for the reader to consider. This is to raise awareness of the issues and to make the reader think. There are useful examples and checklists which can be adapted.

This book does not cover moral and ethical issues.

With regard to terminology, throughout the text for ease of reference, the word 'health professional' is used to include all those involved in healthcare.

The word 'patient' is used to include the patient or the client. The words 'he or she' are used throughout. This is not intended to be derogatory or sexist but simply provides easier reading.

Jane Lynch
August 2010

About the author

Jane Lynch is a practising lawyer specialising in clinical negligence. She was formerly a partner at a City of London firm specialising in clinical negligence. She is on the Law Society's specialist clinical negligence panel and is recognised in the Legal 500 as one of the leading practitioners in England and Wales. She is a consultant for McMillan-Williams Solicitors.

She is a fellow of the Royal Society of Medicine. Jane is also a legal trainer for the health sector and is involved in training National Health Service (NHS) trusts, the private health sector, local authorities, public bodies, professional bodies and the Ministry of Defence (MOD).

She is a regular speaker at international conferences. She also lectures at several universities on the master's degree courses. She has published several papers and articles and is the author of the *Medico-Legal Essentials* series of books. She is well known in the health sector and is very highly regarded in her field.

She is a founding director of the Health Professional Training Agency (www.hpta.co.uk), which specialises in legal training for healthcare professionals.

Acknowledgements

The completion of this work would not have been possible without the support and assistance of a number of people and I am very grateful to all those who contributed to this book. I am particularly grateful to Dr Louise Terry for reading the drafts and providing much appreciated guidance and advice. I am also grateful to Colum Smith and Dr Sue Battersby for painstakingly reading the drafts and reviewing the book.

My gratitude to all those at Radcliffe Publishing and Mia Yardley at Pindar for her kind patience, expertise and guidance during the editing.

To my mother, for her ability to remain positive and energetic throughout the many hours of proof reading. To my daughter Kate. To Michael, Wendy and Hannah for all their support and encouragement.

To my father

CHAPTER 1

Introduction to consent

A patient has the right in law to give or withhold consent to medical examination or treatment. Before a patient can be treated valid consent must be obtained. If the health professional fails to obtain valid consent they will be accountable. This situation may also give rise to civil and criminal proceedings.

For consent to be valid there are many considerations that must be taken into account, such as the patient's age; whether they are a minor; whether they have capacity; whether the risks have been explained; whether they have been given sufficient information; whether they have understood; whether there are language barriers; when the consent was obtained and whether that matters; who obtained consent: and should consent be in writing or can it be verbal or implied?

What makes consent valid? What can invalidate consent?

Litigation is increasing in relation to consent issues. Sadly, not necessarily because valid consent has not been obtained but rather that there is no evidence that valid consent has been obtained. This is because the records are either insufficient in detail or there is nothing recorded. Issues in question often concern what advice was given or which risks were explained. Consent is a complex area in itself and there is often confusion as to when consent issues should be recorded and how it is recorded.

There are many reasons why litigation in respect of clinical care has risen. There have been changes in the law. The Human Rights Act 1998,[1] Data Protection Act 1998[2] and Freedom of Information Act 2000[3] have all impacted on the rights and expectations of the patient. Patients are no longer passive. They are now much more aware of their rights. They have wider access to information, particularly via the Internet. In addition, 'no win, no fee' arrangements in relation to the legal costs of pursuing a claim are widely publicised.

Health professionals must be familiar with the law and must uphold the patient's rights. They must be aware of the issues of consent. The health professional must be aware that they are accountable for their actions.

Before looking at consent in detail it is important for the health professional to understand their legal and professional obligations in the context of consent. Words like civil litigation, negligence, breach of duty and accountability are heard by health professionals but not always understood. This book explains these areas briefly and simply. It also explains the basic court structure to place the legal issues into context. The book then explores the issues of consent in detail.

REFERENCES
1 The Human Rights Act 1998
2 Data Protection Act 1998
3 Freedom of Information Act 2000

CHAPTER 2

The legal process

THE COURT PROCESS

The law, by its nature, applies retrospectively. It is usually when something has gone wrong that the law steps in. We cannot approach the court to ask, 'If I do something in a particular way, will I be in trouble?' In the normal course of events the health professional goes about their daily routine making decisions and weighing up risks. It is hoped that their employer and their professional body will uphold the decisions that are made. When something goes wrong the health professional is accountable.

Where there is failure to obtain valid consent the health professional will be accountable and may become involved in the court process at, for example, an inquest, civil proceedings, criminal proceedings or an employment tribunal.

SOURCES OF LAW

We know the law exists but people do not often think about it when going about their everyday lives even though it is continuously in operation: when goods are bought and sold; when people get married or companies are formed. The law lays down rules in respect of all of these matters. When things are done in the usual way there is little reason to worry. In the normal course of events people only begin to consider the law when some uncertainty or difficulty arises. When a person looks into their situation after a difficulty has arisen they may find it is too late.

Every day decisions are made about patient care, planning and treatment. Terms like 'accountability' and 'responsibility' form part of health professionals' everyday vocabulary, but they do not sit back and think, 'What do they really mean?' However, when something goes wrong they become accountable. Being forewarned is being forearmed and understanding the law and accountability will help health professionals make the right decisions.

The health professional must know the area of law that affects them. For example, those working in mental health should be familiar with the Mental Health Act 1983,[1] the Mental Capacity Act 2005[2] and other legislation. Remember, ignorance of the law is no defence. Health professionals should be aware that the law relating to consent is still evolving. As we speak, changes are still being made in relation to the Mental Capacity Act to redress areas of conflict with other laws. Health professionals have an obligation to keep abreast of any changes.

Very broadly speaking the law is a set of rules. The law in England and Wales is made up of statute and common law. (Common law is sometimes referred to as 'case law'.)

There is no one single act that outlines the law of consent. The law relating to consent is made up of a combination of common law and statute.

STATUTE

A statute is law set out in an Act of Parliament, declaring, commanding, or prohibiting something. It identifies the purpose of the law, how it is to be interpreted, and penalties for failure to adhere to the law and the remedies available to an injured party.

The courts apply statute to the circumstances in determining whether there has been a breach of the law and then apply the penalties.

Statute and consent

Although there is no single statute specifically dealing with consent, there are statutes that impact on and apply to it.

Examples include:

➤ Mental Capacity Act 2005
➤ Human Rights Act 1998[3]
➤ Data Protection Act 1998[4]
➤ Access to Health Records Act 1990[5]

➤ Mental Health Act 1983[1]
➤ Mental Health Act 2007[6]

COMMON LAW (CASE LAW)

Where no statute exists, the courts develop law by considering the particular set of circumstances in a case and making a decision. Those decisions become the law. Hence the term 'case law'. Important decisions, together with reasons for their decisions, are recorded in law reports. These decisions are then followed by the courts when they deal with cases with similar circumstances.

If the common law differs from a statute, the statute will overrule the common law.

An example of what a law report looks like is set out in Box 2.1.

BOX 2.1 JUDGMENTS: CHESTER (RESPONDENT) v
AFSHAR (APPELLANT) 2004[7]

HOUSE OF LORDS   SESSION 2003–04
                                   [2004] UKHL 41
                 on appeal from: [2002] EWCA Civ 724

HOUSE OF LORDS
OPINIONS OF THE LORDS OF APPEAL FOR JUDGMENT
IN THE CAUSE
Chester (Respondent) v Afshar (Appellant)
[2004] UKHL 41
LORD BINGHAM OF CORNHILL

My Lords,

1 The central question in this appeal is whether the conventional approach to causation in negligence actions should be varied where the claim is based on a doctor's negligent failure to warn a patient of a small but unavoidable risk of surgery when, following surgery performed with due care and skill, such risk eventuates but it is not shown that, if duly warned, the patient would not have undergone surgery with the same small but unavoidable risk of mishap. Is it relevant to the outcome of the claim to decide whether, duly

warned, the patient probably would or probably would not have consented to undergo the surgery in question?

2 I am indebted to my noble and learned friend Lord Hope of Craighead for his detailed account of the facts and the history of these proceedings, which I need not repeat.

3 For some six years beginning in 1988 the claimant, Miss Chester, suffered repeated episodes of low back pain. She was conservatively treated by Dr Wright, a consultant rheumatologist, who administered epidural and sclerosant injections. An MRI scan in 1992 showed evidence of disc protrusions. In 1994, on the eve of a professional trip abroad, Miss Chester suffered another episode of pain and disability: she could 'hardly walk', and had reduced control of her bladder. Dr Wright gave another epidural injection, and Miss Chester was able to make the trip, using a wheelchair at Heathrow. But after the trip the pain returned. A further MRI scan revealed marked protrusion of discs into the spinal canal. After further conservative treatment which proved ineffective, Dr Wright referred Miss Chester to Mr Afshar, a distinguished consultant neurosurgeon with much experience of disc surgery, although Miss Chester was understandably reluctant to undergo surgery if this could be avoided.

The case above sets out the requirement in relation to providing information to patients when obtaining consent. This case is discussed in more detail in Chapter 9.

GUIDELINES AND CODES OF PRACTICE

Guidelines, codes of practice, protocols and policies can best be defined as information intended to advise health professionals on how something should be done or what something should be. They are systems of rules and acceptable behaviour.

Guidelines, protocols, policies and codes of practice are set down under legal directives, by professional bodies, regulatory bodies and at local level by the employer. They are laid down for good reason. They provide health professionals with a safe framework for practice. They should be followed as far as is reasonable. However, they should be critically applied and not blindly followed. A good record of how and why any procedure or policy has been departed from should be made. The health professional must justify their actions.

While these codes of practice and guidelines are not legally binding, they are recommended practice. Breaches of them do not usually in themselves give rise to civil or criminal liability (except midwives under the Nursing and Midwifery Council (NMC) *Midwives Rules*).[8] However, a breach may be evidence of failure to follow the approved practice and it could be argued that such breach constituted negligence.

The Department of Health set up the 'Good Practice in Consent' initiative to ensure proper consent is sought from all National Health Service (NHS) patients and research subjects. The plan recognised that a change of culture would be required to ensure that patients become informed partners in their own care. The Department of Health has published guides for health professionals and NHS trusts have incorporated these into their own policies and procedures.

COURT SYSTEM

Where a patient has been treated without valid consent it may give rise to civil or criminal liability.

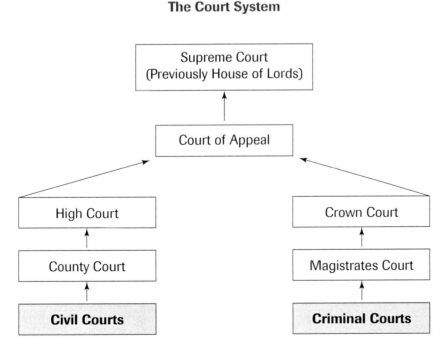

FIGURE 2.1 The court system

Here is a simplified illustration of the court structure. Within the court structure there are a variety of branches not illustrated here such as the Family Division, tribunals or inquiries.

In October 2009, the Supreme Court took over the judicial functions previously performed by the House of Lords. There are some differences between the old and the new courts and all of the Supreme Court's hearings will be open to the public and television cameras will be in court permanently, which is a new step in English legal history (*see* Figure 2.1).

CIVIL LAW

The civil courts deal with civil matters. This can involve money matters, contractual disputes or property issues. They include negligence, trespass to property or the person, nuisance or breach of statutory duty, among other things.

Where a patient has been treated without valid consent the civil matters that concern the health professionals will include:

➤ negligence (a breach of duty of care)
➤ trespass to the person
➤ breach of statutory duty.

Where there has been a breach of the civil law then it may give rise to a claim for compensation by the injured party.

Where a patient has been treated without valid consent this may give rise to a civil claim for compensation.

NEGLIGENCE

Negligence is also referred to as a breach of the duty of care. Failure to obtain consent, or circumstances which arise that may invalidate consent, may give rise to an action in negligence. If a patient is injured as a result of the negligence of a health professional then the patient may sue for financial compensation. (Compensation is also referred to as 'damages'.)

Negligence occurs when the standard of care falls below the reasonable standard expected.

A person who brings a claim for negligence is called the 'claimant' and the person or organisation being sued is called the 'defendant'. The legal process for bringing a claim is often referred to as 'litigation'.

> ### EXAMPLE
>
> Mrs Jones is admitted to hospital for tests. She is required to undergo an endoscopy. She signs the consent form. Following the endoscopy she suffers from bleeding and complains that she was not warned of the risks. She says had she known there was a risk of bleeding she would not have agreed to the endoscopy. She had to stay in hospital longer than expected and was unable to return to work for some weeks.

In these circumstances consent may not be valid because the risks were not explained despite the fact she signed the consent form. She may be entitled to financial compensation for her pain and suffering and loss of earnings.

Duty of Care

There is a duty of care owed by health professionals to obtain valid consent. If consent is not obtained this falls short of what is expected then it may constitute a breach of duty of care. If as a result the patient is injured then it may give rise to a claim for compensation as stated above.

Donoghue v Stevenson 1932

The leading case of Donoghue v Stevenson[9] changed the law relating to negligence and is commonly referred to as the case of 'the snail in the ginger beer'. A claimant who wishes to bring a claim in negligence has to meet the requirements set out by the House of Lords in this case.

FACTS OF THE CASE

Mrs Donoghue and her friend were out shopping and stopped for refreshments. Mrs Donoghue's friend treated Mrs Donoghue to a bottle of ginger beer. Her friend treated her not only to the ginger beer but also to a decomposing snail, which was lurking in the bottom of the bottle. The experience made Mrs Donoghue sick.

Mrs Donoghue sued the café proprietor. The law at this time was based on contractual obligations. The court said Mrs Donoghue had no contract with the café proprietor as it was her friend who had the contract because it was she who had bought the ginger beer. This was sound legal argument at that time and there was no remedy under the law.

So Mrs Donoghue sued the beer manufacturer. The manufacturer's contract was with the café proprietor but the manufacturer did not have a contract with Mrs Donoghue and so she lost again.

The matter then went to the Court of Appeal and it was lost on the same principles. There was no contract between Mrs Donoghue, the ginger beer manufacturer or the café proprietor.

Not content with the outcome, Mrs Donoghue took the matter to the House of Lords. What drove her to do that we will never know!

The House of Lords said that although there was no contract between Mrs Donoghue and the manufacturer, because Mrs Donaghue was affected by the actions of the manufacturer they must owe her a duty of care.

In this case the court set out three principles that must be present in order for a person to succeed in a claim for compensation for negligence:

The three requirements that the claimant must show are:
1 the defendant owed the claimant a duty of care and
2 the defendant breached that duty of care and
3 the defendant's breach of duty caused the damage to the claimant.

The court will determine as a matter of course that a trust or health professional will owe a duty of care to their patient. But the patient then has to show that the duty of care was breached and that the breach caused him damage.

What constitutes a breach of duty?
Bolan v Friern Barnet HMC 1957

The test as to whether health professionals are in breach of their duty of care is whether a responsible body of medical practitioners would have acted in the same way.

A responsible body is judged on the skill of the health professional. 'Where a case involves some special skill or competence then the test as to whether there has been negligence or not is based upon the standard of the ordinary skilled man exercising and professing to have that special skill or knowledge'.[10]

Thus, the negligence of a health professional, say a nurse, will be determined by the standard of the ordinary skilled nurse.

This has the effect that the greater the skill, experience and expertise of the health professional, the greater the duty of care. For example, a specialist nurse will owe a greater duty than a non-specialist nurse.

Standard of proof

In the civil courts the standard of proof is 'on the balance of probablity'. The court will ask, 'is it more likely than not that a certain set of circumstances occurred?'

In civil cases it is up to the claimant to prove their case.

EXAMPLE

A female patient attends hospital complaining of severe stomach cramps. She is examined and an ectopic pregnancy is suspected. The doctor informs the patient that they need to take her to theatre as soon as possible to check if it is an ectopic pregnancy and to remove the fetus if it is necessary. The patient is given a pre-med and taken to theatre. Consent is then discussed with the patient and the doctor mentions that they may need to carry out a hysterectomy. The patient is given the consent form to sign.

The patient returns from theatre to discover that the fetus has not survived and a hysterectomy has been carried out. There is now no prospect of her ever having children.

The questions then are:

Consent issues
➤ Was valid consent obtained?
➤ Were the risks advised?
➤ Were there any circumstances that may invalidate consent?

Duty-of-care issues
➤ Was there a duty of care regarding the way consent was obtained?
➤ Did the defendant breach the duty of care? Would a responsible body of medical practitioners have acted in the same way?
➤ Did the breach of duty of care cause the damage to the patient?

Obtaining consent of the patient after the pre-med has been administered is likely to invalidate consent as it could be argued that the patient did not have capacity to agree to the procedure. Explaining the possible need to undergo the hysterectomy so soon before the procedure is likely to invalidate consent as the patient will not have had sufficient time to consider the information in order to reach a decision. Unless the hysterectomy was carried out in an emergency and in order to save her life, it is likely that the health professional will be in breach of duty of care. If the patient had been fully informed about the hysterectomy she would have refused such procedure. She has now suffered, as she is unable to have any children. The breach of duty of care caused this suffering. The patient may succeed in a claim for compensation.

CRIMINAL LAW

Criminal courts deal with criminal matters. Situations giving rise to criminal charges in relation to healthcare may include deliberate harm to a patient, for example, cases such as Beverly Allitt[11] and Harold Shipman,[12] who killed some their patients; Colin Norris[13] who was convicted of the murder of four patients and Barbara Salisbury[14] who was jailed for five years in 2004 for the attempted murder of two patients. Other criminal matters may include manslaughter for gross negligence or recklessness, assault and battery, fraud or theft.

Deliberate harm caused

Of course, it is rare that a health professional intends to cause harm to a patient. In the usual course of events the health professional does not intend to cause deliberate harm. Where a patient dies as a result of treatment that was grossly negligent this can constitute manslaughter. The case of R v Adomako is an example.[15]

R v Adomako 1994

This case involved manslaughter by an anaesthetist when during surgery the endotrachael tube disconnected and this went unnoticed by the anaesthetist. The supply of oxygen to the patient ceased which led to cardiac arrest and death.

The anaesthetist first became aware that something was wrong when the alarm sounded on the Dinamap machine, which monitors the patient's blood pressure. The evidence was that almost 5 minutes had elapsed between the disconnection and the alarm sounding. Following the alarm the anaesthetist responded in various ways by checking the equipment and administering atropine to raise the patient's blood pressure. But at no stage before the cardiac arrest did the anaesthetist check the endotrachael tube connection. The disconnection was not discovered until after resuscitation measures had commenced.

This was considered to be so reckless and grossly negligent that it constituted manslaughter.

Assault and battery

A health professional may commit a common law criminal offence of assault and battery if they treat a patient without valid consent.

Assault and battery are both common law and statutory offences. Under the common law they are two different offences.

Assault is 'any act by which a person intentionally or recklessly causes another person to apprehend immediate and unlawful personal violence'.

Battery is 'any act by which a person, intentionally or recklessly inflicts unlawful personal violence upon another person'.

Section 42 and section 47 of the Offences Against the Persons Act 1861 (OAPA)[16,17] states that a person committing any common assault or battery may be imprisoned or compelled to pay fines and costs. Section 42, therefore, implies that there are offences committed either when someone is put in fear of unlawful violence (assault) or when there is an unlawful application of force to the person of another (battery).

In reality, common assault is only used in situations where a blow or another application of force is struck, but when no actual injury results.

Section 47 of the OAPA is concerned with assault occasioning 'actual bodily harm'. The assault may or may not include battery in the sense of actual contact with the victim, i.e. if someone strikes another with their fist causing injury, this will be an assault causing actual bodily harm, as will striking a horse with a whip causing the rider to fall and injure themselves. Actual bodily harm simply means some bodily harm.

Section 20 of the OAPA 1861[18] is concerned with unlawfully and maliciously wounding or inflicting any grievous bodily harm upon another person. Unlawfully simply means without lawful excuse.

There are three possible lawful excuses, namely:
➤ self-defence
➤ accident
➤ consent.

If any of these three ingredients are present then the defendant has a good defence in law.

Put simply:

➤ An assault is the fear or apprehension of being struck. For example, it is the nurse lunging forward with the syringe.

➤ Battery is the physical contact. It is when the syringe physically touches and punctures the skin.

It could be argued that if the health professional crept up to the patient from behind and gave the injection, there would be a battery but no assault. However, this is not to be recommended!

EXAMPLE

A mother with her son of 8 years and daughter of 7 years attended the dentist. An appointment had been made only for the mother and daughter. While in the waiting room the son went to the bathroom. He was missing for about 15 minutes when his mother became worried. She went to look for him and found him in the dentist chair. Her son had been seen in the corridor by the dentist, who said, 'Come on, chappy in the chair'. The dentist then proceeded to give him the treatment that was intended for the daughter. The dentist extracted two second molars.

This constituted not only a breach of duty of care but also an assault, as there was no consent.

Where valid consent has been obtained this is a defence to an assault and battery.

Touching the patient

Assault and battery must be distinguished from touching a patient. Health professionals sometimes abandon a patient who needs compassion because they are afraid to extend humanity for fear of being sued for unconsented touching. It is okay to touch a patient to extend compassion, for example, by a touch on the arm or hand – this will not be battery. Health professionals must, however, be alert to signals that the patient does not want to be touched.

Standard of proof

In criminal cases the burden of proof is 'beyond all reasonable doubt'. The jury must be sure of the guilt of the defendant. The standard of proof is higher in criminal cases because somebody's liberty is at stake. So, the court has to be sure that an offence had been committed.

It is the prosecution's duty to prove their case against the defendant. Penalties for common assault include a financial fine of up to £5000 and/or 6 months custody.

The court will also consider compensation payment by the defendant to the victim.[21]

REFERENCES

 1 The Mental Health Act 1983
 2 Mental Capacity Act 2005
 3 Human Rights Act 1998
 4 Data Protection Act 1998
 5 Access to Health Records Act 1990
 6 The Mental Health Act 2007
 7 Chester v Afshar [2004] UKHL 41; [2005] 1 AC 134; [2004] 3 WLR 927; [2004] 4 All ER 587
 8 Nursing and Midwifery Council. *Midwives Rules and Standards* 05.04. London: Nursing and Midwifery Council; 2004. Available at: www.nmc-uk.org/Documents/Standards/nmcMidwivesRulesandStandards.pdf (accessed 30 June 2010).
 9 Donoghue v Stevenson [1932] All ER
10 Bolam v Friern Barnet HMC [1957] 2 All ER 118
11 R v Beverly Allitt 1992
12 R v Harold Shipman 2000
13 R v Colin Norris 2008
14 R v Barbara Salisbury 2004
15 R v Adomako [1995] 1AC 171 23; [1994] 3 All ER 79
16 Offences Against the Persons Act 1861, s42
17 Offences Against the Persons Act 1861, s47
18 Offences Against the Persons Act 1861, s20
19 Criminal Justice Act 1988, s39

CHAPTER 3

Accountability

> 'I would have explained the risks to my patient, I usually do, I acted in good faith.'

The ethos in healthcare has changed over the past few years. The days when a doctor was put on a pedestal not to be challenged are gone. Now we live in a very different environment. Patients are much more aware of their rights. Patients are more informed which has increased with access to the Internet. The law has changed and this has impacted upon health professionals. The Human Rights Act 1998[1] and the Mental Capacity Act 2005[2] to name but a few have impacted upon the way health professionals care for patients.

For health professionals such changes mean that the law has become part of their role and is now an everyday concern. The complexities of the law do not make this an easy task for them. In a healthcare setting it leaves the health professionals vulnerable. In practice they go about their daily routines, making decisions about patient care, planning and treating, and it is hoped that the right decisions are made, that their employer will stand by them and courts will uphold the decisions of the health professional.

Health professionals have concerns about who is responsible when a patient suffers harm. Can a health professional be held accountable where they have no control over the preparation of standard forms such as consent forms, resources or they are ignorant through lack of training?

Health professionals are often heard in the witness box saying, 'Staff were under pressure, but I meant well'.

Of course health professionals do not intend to cause harm, they may have no control over resources, may be ignorant of procedures through lack of training. However, this does not exonerate the health professional from their responsibility, when something goes awry they are accountable.

It is important for health professionals to be aware of their legal and professional obligations but also to put them into perspective – getting the balance right. Often health professionals have an unhealthy fear of the law, causing unnecessary anxiety. This approach must be balanced with an unrealistic view that it will never happen to them, that someone else or something else is responsible, 'but not me'. Often a defensive approach is adopted. 'I don't have the time', 'it's because of financial constraints', 'it's my manager's responsibility' or 'it's the consultant's responsibility'. The health professional cannot simply pass responsibility like a hot potato, they will be accountable for their actions.

My intention is not to alarm the health professional but to impart the information realistically in a way that a balance may be struck.

The concept of accountability is one which is familiar to all health professionals. It is a word which they all know and use and forms part of their working day vocabulary. But how can it be defined?

TASK

1   Before you read further try to define 'accountability'
2   List the areas where you think you are accountable

TASK

A patient is to undergo surgery. A Senior House Officer (SHO) is told by the consultant to get the patient to sign the consent form. The patient asks the SHO questions about the procedure. The SHO explains the known risks and is able to answer most of the questions. The patient signs the consent form. The patient suffers an adverse reaction due to his underlying heart condition. The patient says the SHO did not mention this risk. The patient would not have had the surgery if he had known about the risk.

Think about this situation and consider:
1   Who is accountable?
2   To whom are they accountable?

Read on and we will then review the scenario.

Accountability in a legal context

In a legal context there is no distinction between responsibility and accountability. Responsibility can be defined as being accountable for, answerable for, liable to be called to account.

The reality of the situation is that a health professional is, on a personal level, answerable and can be called to account. Once that premise has been accepted, the inevitable and consequent enquiry which must flow from that is to whom and how is that accountability discharged? How far the health professional can be held accountable for their actions is not within the ambit of this book.[3]

The discharge of the duty is debated by, and lies with, the courts. The law by its nature is reactive and is invoked after the event. It is only when a real case is presented that the judges will deliberate and deliver judgment. It follows that issues are debated with the benefit of hindsight. Therefore we cannot go to the courts with hypothetical questions or scenarios – to ask 'If I do it in particular way, will I be in trouble?' The usual sequence is that something will have happened to trigger an investigation. This will raise the question of accountability. When the health professional appears before the court his acts or omissions will be weighed up and judgment will be delivered. The practical effect is that health professionals make decisions about patient care and it is hoped that the courts will ultimately support them.

Accountability has now been put into its legal context. The next question then is: to whom is the health professional accountable?

TASK

■ To whom is the health professional accountable?

List them

THE FOUR AREAS OF ACCOUNTABILITY

There is not just a single individual or body to whom the health professional is accountable but four separate and distinct areas in which they are answerable. In the widest sense, the health professional is answerable to society. Perhaps, and more important from the health professional's perspective, he must be accountable and answerable to the patient. Equally, the health professional will be answerable to his employer and last but certainly not least, the health professional will also be accountable to his profession.

Having established that the health professional can be accountable in four quite separate and distinct respects, we need next to examine how accountability impacts in practice.

1 Society

Health professionals are accountable to society for issues that are in the public interest. Society dictates the kind of behaviour they will and will not accept. If someone is murdered society says this is wrong and the murderer must be punished. Society's view is then enshrined in criminal law. We have seen manslaughter charges brought against school teachers where a child has died on a school trip. These charges are brought because the teachers have not lived up to the trust society imposes. It will be argued that the individual has fallen short of what society accepts and demands of someone in that position. If found guilty they face a penalty. As society changes then the law may change to reflect these changes in society's values. For example, suicide used to be considered a crime but is no longer and the law changed to reflect this.

It has already been mentioned that failing to obtain consent before treating a patient constitutes a criminal offence.

When dealing with accountability to society the discharge of such accountability rests with the criminal courts. The criminal court acts in the public interest. The prosecutor derives no benefit.

Criminal proceedings are brought against an individual. It is personal. It is not possible for the individual to be indemnified by the employer or defence union. The health professional's boss is not going to say, 'don't worry I'll serve your sentence for you'!

In a case involving a major motor company an employee died having fallen into a vat of paint and drowned. The director was found guilty and fined £5000 personally. The court made it clear this was to be paid by the director personally and not to be paid by the company.

The kind of sanctions that may be imposed by the criminal courts include:

➤ Custodial sentence – imprisonment
➤ Fine
➤ Community-based sentences.

Any criminal conviction is reported to the professional body of a health professional.

2 Patient

Health professionals are accountable to the patient or client. The discharge of accountability rests with the civil courts. Civil law is not about punishment, unlike the criminal process. If a patient is injured as a result of negligent treatment the patient may seek financial compensation through the civil courts. The purpose of the patient suing for compensation is to put them back into the position they would have been in financially, if the incident had not occurred.

EXAMPLE

A patient attends hospital as a day patient for the removal of a polyp under general anaesthetic. Due to an error with the records the patient is added to the wrong theatre list and instead of carrying out the removal of the polyp the patient's leg is amputated by mistake. The patient sues for compensation for financial loss. Had the correct procedure been carried out the patient would have had the polyp removed and then been discharged that day. He would have returned to work and usual daily life. However the patient's condition is now such that he has to stay in hospital, cannot return to work so has lost his income, will require care at home, equipment and further treatment which he will now have to pay for. The damages the patient claims are to recompense him for this financial loss. There will also be some recompense for pain and suffering.

The value of such claims will vary as it is based on the loss endured by the individual. Therefore the same circumstances may arise with two patients but one claim may be valued at £5000 whereas the other might be valued at £5 million. The difference is that if the first patient was unemployed at the time of the incident and never likely to work in any event then there is no claim for loss of earnings. Whereas the second patient may be a professional footballer at the peak of his career and therefore the loss of earnings could be very substantial.

3 Employer

If a patient has been injured as a result of a failure to obtain valid consent constituting negligence, the patient may sue for compensation. Who does the patient sue, the individual health professional or the employer, for example the Trust?

Vicarious liability

Some employers accept liability for negligent acts and/or omissions by their employees. This is known as vicarious liability. Such cover does not normally extend to activities undertaken outside the health professional's employment. Independent practice would not normally be covered by vicarious liability.

If a health professional is self-employed or works in the private health sector it is the individual health professional's responsibility to establish their insurance status and take appropriate action. In situations where employers do not accept vicarious liability, then it is recommended that health professionals should obtain adequate professional indemnity insurance. If a health professional is unable to secure professional indemnity insurance, then they will need to demonstrate that all their clients/patients are fully informed of this fact and the implications this might have in the event of a claim for professional negligence.

Where the employer is vicariously liable for the employee they are liable for their acts and omissions. It does not matter whether the employee is full time, part time, temporary or agency staff, they will be considered to be acting as an agent for the Trust. In practical terms this means the Trust is responsible for the actions of their employees. It therefore follows that although the individual health professional may have been negligent, any claim for compensation will be met by the employer. While there is nothing in law preventing the patient suing the individual health professional the patient will usually choose to sue the Trust rather than the individual. This is because the Trust is more likely to have the financial resources to pay the compensation. There is no point is suing a man of straw (someone with no money). Thus the health professionals concerned in the incident do not themselves have to pay the compensation.

There are, however, exceptions to this. The Trust may in certain circumstances recoup the compensation they have paid out from the individuals concerned in the incident. This should only be pursued in exceptional circumstances. Exceptional circumstances are likely to include causing deliberate harm, such as in the Beverly Allitt[4] case. However, the Nursing and Midwifery Council (NMC)[5] make it clear that where a nurse prescribes outsides her powers then the Trust may not stand by them. Therefore it is recommended that health professionals have indemnity insurance in place.

The Trust sought to recover from Allitt the compensation they had paid out to her victims. In reality, of course the Trust is unlikely to recover the compensation from her because she is in prison, has no income and is therefore unlikely to have the resources to pay back the money. One of the reasons why a Trust may seek to recover such compensation is because of public perception. They do not want the public to think that they are condoning this kind of behaviour.

Notwithstanding that it is the Trust, not the individual that will be sued and that it is the Trust that will pay out the compensation, this does not exonerate the health professionals and they are still accountable to their employer.

The employer may be unhappy about what has happened and it is open to the employer to look into the matter. The employer will be concerned with the contract of employment and whether there has been any breach of that contract, and whether the employee has acted outside their job description.

EXAMPLE

A district nurse who for many years worked in community care took up a new post with in an accident and emergency department. The standard job description was that only a doctor can suture hands and face. A patient was admitted whose face required suturing. The nurse considered herself far more experienced than the junior doctors and so she did suture the patient's face. It all went wrong and the patient was left with scarring that could have been avoided. The employer considered that the nurse was in breach of her contract of employment. The job description was clear. According to the job description she was prohibited from suturing a patient's face. The employer dismissed the nurse from employment.

It is implied in a contract of employment that an employee will obey reasonable instructions of the employer and that the employee will use all their care and skill in carrying out their duties. As an employee the health professional cannot embark on a 'frolic of their own'. They are answerable to the employer and it is open to the employer to look at it and address it.

The kind of sanctions the employer can invoke are:

➤ grievance procedure
➤ disciplinary procedure.

This could lead to:

➤ warning
➤ demotion
➤ suspension
➤ dismissal.

4 Professional body

Health professionals are answerable to their employer – this may result in disciplinary action with sanctions. The ultimate sanction being dismissal.

Professional bodies regulate health professionals. Their primary aim is to protect the public. This is achieved by setting and maintaining standards of education, training, conduct and performance that the public is entitled to expect. These are usually set out in their codes of conduct.

Professional bodies will look at whether the health professional has maintained their professional duty.

It is the responsibility of the health professionals to be familiar with their codes of conduct and the duties of a health professional.

The professional body will look at whether the health professional is competent to practise, whether they are safe, whether they have maintained professional standards and so on.

Information about a health professional may be received by the professional body from a number of sources. Anyone has the right to make a complaint. If there is a criminal conviction it will be reported to the professional body. Non-criminal misconduct may also be reported. A health professional may be referred by a judge following a civil court hearing. The police may report the conduct of a health professional. A patient or their family, their employer, managers and colleagues, or other health professionals may report them. The professional body will then investigate the matter and this may then result in a hearing before a conduct and competence committee to decide the case.

There are many regulatory bodies governing healthcare. They include, for example:

➤ Nursing and Midwifery Council (NMC)[6]
➤ General Medical Council (GMC)[7]

- General Dental Council (GDC)[8]
- General Chiropractic Council (GCC)[9]
- General Optical Council (GOC)[10]
- Royal Pharmaceutical Society of Great Britain (RPSGB)[11]
- Health Professions Council (HPC).[12]

These professional bodies will be concerned with issues surrounding fitness to practise and the health professional's suitability to be on the register without restrictions. They will consider whether the health professional's fitness to practise is impaired. Issues that can impair this include:
- lack of competence
- physical or mental ill health
- misconduct
- a finding by any other health or social care regulator or licensing body that a registrant's fitness to practise is impaired
- a conviction or caution (including a finding of guilt by a court martial)
- fraudulent or incorrect entry in the professional register.

Sanctions that can be imposed by a professional body

There are sanctions that can be imposed by the professional bodies. The purpose of such sanctions is not to punish the health professional but to protect the public.

The kind of sanctions that can be imposed include:
- a conditions of practice order. For example, they may impose conditions the health professional must comply with such as they may require them to undertake training or work with supervision
- a caution order
- a suspension order
- a striking off order.

Health professionals need also to be aware that regulatory bodies can look outside what they do in their professional roles to assess whether they are fit to practise.

The NMC guidelines state that:

> You must behave in a way that upholds the reputation of the professions. Behaviour that compromises this reputation may call your registration into question even if is not directly connected to your professional practice.

An example was a health professional who was removed from the register for soliciting a woman for prostitution.

With regard to consent, a health professional can be called into question as to their fitness to practise for failing to obtain valid consent.

The healthcare professional can be called to account in all four areas of accountability which means in effect they can be tried four times.

The case of Beverly Allitt is an illustration of this.[13]

> **Society** – Beverly Allitt was accountable to society. She was considered to have failed society, killing and injuring children, committing criminal offences. For this she was prosecuted in the criminal courts and a custodial sentence was imposed.

> **Patient** – Beverly Allitt was accountable to her patients. The parents of the deceased and injured children brought civil claims for compensation and the Trust paid out compensation.

> **Employer** – Her employers pursued disciplinary proceedings against her and she was dismissed from her employment.

> **Professional body** – The professional body removed her from the register.

It is important for health professionals to appreciate that the four areas of accountability are separate and distinct. Where, for example, due to lack of resources the Trust condones or turns a blind eye to the carrying out of duties that are beyond the skill of the health professional, the Trust may decide to take no disciplinary action. However, the Trust cannot protect the health professional from the other areas of accountability. So, if the patient was harmed despite the Trust having turned a blind eye the patient can still sue, criminal charges can be brought against the health professionals and the professional body can step in. It is no defence for the health professional to say the Trust knew about it. The health professional will still be held accountable for their actions.

It does not necessarily follow that if an employer dismisses the health professional, the professional body will strike a health professional from the register.

Nor does it necessarily follow that if the professional body strikes someone from the register, they will be dismissed from their employment. However, in these circumstances the health professional concerned would lose their registered position.

REFERENCES

1 Human Rights Act 1998
2 Mental Capacity Act 2005
3 Further reading: Lynch J. *Clinical Responsibility*. Medico-Legal Essentials. Oxford: Radcliffe; 2009.
4 R v Beverly Allitt 1992
5 Nursing and Midwifery Council
6 Nursing and Midwifery Council
7 General Medical Council
8 General Dental Council
9 General Chiropractic Council
10 General Optical Council
11 Royal Pharmaceutical Society of Great Britain
12 Health Professions Council
13 R v Beverly Allitt 1992

CHAPTER 4

The basic principles of consent

WHY IS IT NECESSARY TO HAVE CONSENT?

The law states that consent must be obtained from the patient before commencing treatment, physical investigation or personal care. Obtaining consent is also a fundamental part of good practice and good patient care. A patient has the right in law to give or withhold consent to medical examination or treatment. If a patient has not consented to treatment the health professional will be accountable. It is important for health professionals to understand their legal and professional obligations, how they apply in practice and what the consequences are of getting them wrong.

In order for consent to be valid there are many considerations to be borne in mind such as the age of the patient, whether they have capacity, how much time has lapsed between consent and the treatment and informing the patient of risks, among other things.

Failure to apply the appropriate principles may result in treating a patient without valid consent or may result in consent becoming invalid at some later time. If a patient has not consented to treatment a health professional may be guilty of trespass or battery and will be accountable in other areas. Poor handling of the consent process may also result in complaints from patients through the complaints procedure or the professional bodies.

Consent is a complex issue and it is hardly surprising that health professionals may unintentionally treat a patient without valid consent, nevertheless the health professional will be accountable.

THE RIGHT OF SELF-DETERMINATION

Consent is a fundamental right enjoyed by the patient. It is the patient's right to give or withhold consent to medical examination or treatment. It is up to the patient what happens to his or her own body.

The courts have ruled that a mentally competent adult has an absolute right to refuse or to consent to medical treatment for any reason whether rational or irrational, or for no reason at all, even where the decision may lead to the patient's own death or that of their unborn child. No one else, not even next of kin, can consent on behalf of a competent adult.

Re MB 1997

In the case of Re MB the judge stated

> A mentally competent patient has an absolute right to refuse to consent to medical treatment for any reason, rational or irrational, or for no reason at all, even where that decision may lead to his or her own death.[1]

The effect of this case is that a patient who is mentally competent to make a treatment decision may choose not to have medical intervention, even though the consequences may be the death or serious handicap of the child she bears, or even her own death. This principle extends to all patients. When a competent adult refuses treatment the court does not have jurisdiction to declare medical intervention lawful.

This concept must be grasped at the outset. It may seem obvious and simple to apply. However, in practice there is often an inherent conflict of interest where the treatment offered is refused to the detriment of the patient. The ethos of the health professional is pro life, however, this principle cannot override the wishes of a competent patient. When a patient refuses treatment the health professional sometimes struggles to uphold it. Where, for example, a patient refuses a procedure which could be life saving, such as receiving insulin, a blood transfusion or a caesarean section, there is a temptation to find a way to treat the patient. They will ask a psychiatrist to determine that the patient lacks capacity or they will ask family members for consent to proceed, they will say the patient came into the hospital therefore it is implied that they want to be treated. The law does not uphold this.

There are sometimes financial considerations such as a patient who refuses simple treatment for diabetes, as a result of refusal to accept, the cost of alternative care required increases enormously and puts financial pressure on the health providers. While this is frustrating such financial implications cannot override the basic principles of the patient's right to decide.

The basic principle that it is 'up to the patient' must be applied. There are, however, limited exceptions to this such as minors or those who lack capacity. These will be dealt with later but the basic principle must always be the starting point. For clarity this book looks at the basic principles first and then looks at the exceptions which may then apply.

Another important point to remember at the outset is that an adult is presumed to have capacity unless the health professional can show otherwise.

TASK

The unborn child
Susan wishes to have a natural birth. She has made it clear to the midwife she does not want to have a caesarean section. But without a caesarean section the baby will die.

Does the midwife have an obligation to save the unborn child regardless of the patient's consent?

The unborn child is not considered in law to be a legal entity until it is born. Therefore, if a pregnant mother refuses treatment she cannot be compelled on the basis of saving the unborn child. Remember the basic principles of Re MB.[1] It is up to the patient what happens to their own body. As the child is not yet born it is considered part of the mother's body.

The law relating to consent has the effect that you cannot compel the patient to undergo treatment if they are a competent adult. Health professionals should work in partnership with the mother to ensure she is clear about the circumstances and risks to her unborn baby. Remember refusal of the caesarean section does not mean that the mother lacks capacity, but if there is any question over the mother's capacity the rules relating to this under the MCA must be adhered to.

WORKING IN PARTNERSHIP

When seeking consent the health professional and the patient should work in partnership. The relationship may be described as 'joint decision-making'. The patient and health professional come to an agreement on the best way forward, based on the patient's values and preferences and the health professional's clinical knowledge.

It is important for health professionals to work with the patient, not to make a decision for them but to assist them in the decision process. Providing information, and discussing any concerns the patient may have so they can make their decision.

The General Medical Council (GMC) in their guidelines for doctors states:

> You must work in partnership with your patients. You should discuss with them their condition and treatment options in a way they can understand, and respect their right to make decisions about their care. You should see getting their consent as an important part of the process of discussion and decision-making, rather than as something that happens in isolation.[2]

EXAMPLE

A patient refuses treatment for cancer. His reason is that his father died of cancer. His treatment was not successful, was painful and distressing and he does not want to die in the same way. He could not cope with the treatment and would rather a better quality of life, even if it is shortened as a result.

However, his father may have had a different form of cancer, treatment may be different and the prognosis might be better.

Working in partnership with the patient will allow the patient to the explore these kind of issues and reach an informed decision.

It should be noted, however, that a patient does not have to give a reason. This is the patient's choice. This is explored further ante.

VOLUNTARY AND WITHOUT DURESS OR FRAUD

It is a fundamental principle that consent must be given freely. In order for consent to be valid it must be given by the patient voluntarily without duress or fraud. There must be no pressure or undue influence being exerted on the patient either to accept or refuse treatment.

Where consent is obtained under pressure or undue influence it will be invalid.

Under pressure

Patients may be put under pressure by a spouse, partners, family members, employers, insurers as well as health professionals or carers. Health professionals should be alert to this possibility and where appropriate should arrange to see the patient on their own to establish that the decision is truly that of the patient.

Pressures from family must not override the rights of the patient. An example is where the ambulance service are put under pressure by worried family members to take their mother with breathing difficulties into hospital, where the patient themselves do not wish to go. They are at the end of their life and they would rather die in the chair with the cat curled up on their lap, than in a hospital environment. It is often a concern that if the ambulance crew do not take the patient to hospital they will face a complaint or legal claim by the family.

In practice, this is a difficult situation but remember the basic principle that it is up to the patient. If the patient has not consented to such actions then the ambulance crew are accountable for treating the patient without valid consent.

Other circumstances where pressure may be exerted are where there are cultural issues or pressure by a partner or parent to undergo, for example, a termination of pregnancy. Pressure from worried family to undergo life-saving treatment notwithstanding the patient may not want it. It can be difficult for health professionals to deal with family members and there is a temptation for the health professional to succumb to the pressures of the family to treat the patient regardless of the patient's refusal.

Pressure from health professionals is a particular issue where the ethos of pro-life conflicts with the patient's right of self-determination. Where a patient refuses treatment there is a temptation to try to find a way around consent. It is often very difficult for a health professional to stand back and watch a patient die when intervention could save them. Remember the basic principle, it is up to the patient.

You should also be aware of other situations in which patients may be vulnerable and thus susceptible to pressure, for example, if they are resident in a care home, subject to mental health legislation, detained by the police or immigration services, or in prison.

Health professionals use their specialist knowledge and experience and clinical judgment, and the patient's views and understanding of their condition, to identify which investigations or treatments are likely to result in overall benefit for the patient. The health professional explains the options to the patient, setting out the potential benefits, risks, burdens and side-effects of each option, including the option to have no treatment. The health professional may recommend a particular option which they believe to be best for the patient, but they must not put pressure on the patient to accept their advice.

A health professional must not impose their own value judgments. This will invalidate consent. The health professional must always act in the best interest of the patient.

A patient will make a decision based on their own reasons and values. Remember the decision is the patient's right. It does not matter if their reason is irrational and a health professional must not confer their own values or beliefs on a patient.

Coercion

Freeman v Home Office

> A prisoner challenged the legality of a being injected with drugs for a personality disorder on the basis that he had not given consent and that being given medicine by a doctor in a custodial situation precluded consent being given voluntarily.
>
> The Court stated 'where in a prison setting a doctor has the power to influence a prisoners situation and prospects, a court must be alive to the risks of what may appear on the face of it to be real consent, is not in fact so'.[3]

When patients are seen and treated in environments where involuntary detention may be an issue, such as prisons and mental health units, there is a potential for treatment offered to be perceived as coercive.

Threats such as withdrawal of privileges or loss of remission of sentence for refusing consent, or using such matters to induce consent is likely to be perceived as coercion.

Coercion should be distinguished from providing the patient with appropriate reassurance concerning their treatment, or pointing out the potential benefits of treatment.

Coercion invalidates consent and care must be taken to ensure that the patient makes a decision freely.

Acquiescence

Acquiescence where the person gives in or does not know what the intervention entails is not consent.

A patient who simply gives in who, for example, says 'I don't really want it, but go ahead then', is acquiescing and this is not valid consent.

REFERENCES

1 Re MB [1997] 2 FLR 426
2 General Medical Council (GMC). *Consent: patients and doctors making decisions together.* London: General Medical Council; 2008. p. 5.
3 Freeman v Home Office [1984] 1 QB 524

CHAPTER 5

Scope of consent

It is important to ensure that the health professional obtains consent for the procedure that is actually being undertaken. For example, do not assume that consent for a colonoscopy includes consent to remove tissue while undertaking the procedure. If it is anticipated that tissue may be removed during the procedure then specific consent for the removal of tissue must also be obtained. The patient must be given information about the removal of tissue, risks, etc. so they can make a decision as to whether they wish to proceed.

Health professionals, for example, pathologists and radiologists may on occasions encounter uncertainty about a diagnosis which can only be resolved by investigations which were not specifically ordered as part of the original request for testing. If these investigations appear to fall outside the scope of the original consent given by the patient, or there are particular sensitivities around the condition for which the pathologist or radiologist wishes to test, they must contact the treating health professional and establish whether further discussion with, and consent from, the patient is necessary before proceeding.

Where the patient agrees to only parts of a proposed plan, the health professional should make sure that there is a clear process through which they can be involved in making decisions at a later stage.

Health professionals must not exceed the scope of the authority given by a patient, except in an emergency. Acting in an emergency is discussed in detail in Chapter 16.

SEEKING CONSENT

Who should obtain consent?

The health professional carrying out the treatment, investigation or care is responsible for ensuring that the patient has given valid consent before treatment begins.

Delegation

A doctor responsible for the patient's care will remain ultimately responsible for the quality of clinical care provided. When seeking consent the treating doctor is responsible for obtaining patient consent. It can, however, be delegated to another health professional, as long as that professional is suitably trained and qualified, has sufficient knowledge of the proposed investigation or treatment and understands the risks involved in order to be able to provide any information the patient may require. The doctor who delegates remains responsible and must make sure that the patient has been given enough time and information to make an informed decision, and has given their consent, before the investigation or treatment is commenced. The same principles apply to health professionals such as a nurse who delegates to a healthcare assistant.

Inappropriate delegation (for example, where the health professional seeking consent has inadequate knowledge of the procedure) may mean that the 'consent' obtained is not valid. Health professionals are responsible for knowing the limits of their own competence and should seek the advice of appropriate colleagues when necessary.

Circumstances exist, for example, in General Practitioner (GP) surgeries, where the receptionist will provide the patient with a consent form to sign before proceeding to the GP or practice nurse for the treatment. This is not appropriate and the GP or nurse carrying out the procedure must ensure that valid consent has been obtained. A signature on the form alone is not sufficient to constitute valid consent.

When should consent be obtained?

Seeking and giving consent is usually an ongoing process, rather than a one-off event.

Each time treatment is carried out consent should be obtained.

EXAMPLE

Mary has a broken hip and has consented to surgery. She has signed the consent form. There is a delay of 3 days before surgery takes place. In the meantime a care plan has been discussed and agreed with her and she is treated conservatively with bed rest and pain relief. Although consent for both surgery and the care plan has been agreed, consent is nevertheless an ongoing process. Each time care is provided consent must be obtained. This can be done simply by stating 'I am going to give you your tablets now', 'It is time for your surgery, is there anything you would like to ask'. The patient has already consented to this but remember consent is ongoing and therefore it is good practice to inform the patient what it is you are doing so as to reconfirm their consent and to give them the opportunity to withdraw it.

Before commencing treatment, the health professional should check that the patient still wants to go ahead; and must respond to any new or repeated concerns or questions they raise. This is particularly important if: significant time has passed since the initial decision was made, there have been material changes in the patient's condition, or in any aspect of the proposed investigation or treatment or new information has become available, for example, about the risks of treatment or about other treatment options.

The patient must be kept informed about the progress of their treatment, and make decisions at all stages, not just in the initial stage. If the treatment is ongoing, the health professional should make sure that there are clear arrangements in place to review decisions and, if necessary, to make new ones.

Well in advance

For major interventions, it is good practice where possible to seek the patient's consent to the proposed procedure well in advance, when there is time to respond to the patient's questions and provide sufficient information.

If consent is obtained well in advance the health professional should check, before the procedure starts, that the patient still consents. If a patient is not asked to signify their consent until just before the procedure is due to start, at a time when they may be feeling particularly vulnerable, there may be real doubt as to its validity.

Shortly prior to the procedure

Consent is sometimes obtained shortly before the procedure commences. There is a danger that consent in these circumstances may be invalid. Patients should not be given routine pre-operative medication before being asked for their consent to proceed with the treatment as this may impact on their capacity.

It is not appropriate to say to a patient as they are being wheeled into theatre 'by the way can we remove your kidney if we need to'. This would not be valid. The consequences of a nephrectomy are significant and the patient must be given sufficient information and sufficient time to consider it before making a decision (this is different to an emergency situation which is discussed later).

It may, however, be reasonable to obtain consent from a patient shortly before the procedure where, for example, a health professional is taking a patient's blood pressure.

HOW LONG DOES CONSENT LAST?

When a patient gives valid consent to treatment, that consent may remain valid indefinitely unless it is withdrawn by the patient or there are changes to the patient's condition, treatment plan or options. If new information becomes available regarding the proposed treatment, for example, new evidence of risks or new treatment options arise between the time when consent was sought and when the intervention is undertaken the health professional should inform the patient and reconfirm their consent.

The health professional should consider whether the new information should be drawn to the attention of the patient and the process of seeking consent repeated on the basis of this information. Similarly, if the patient's condition has changed significantly in the intervening time, it may be necessary to seek consent again, on the basis that the likely benefits and/or risks of the intervention may also have changed.

If consent has been obtained a significant time before undertaking the intervention, it is good practice to confirm that the person who has given consent still wishes the intervention to proceed even if no new information needs to be provided or further questions answered.

PATIENT CHOICE

'Patient choice' is a phrase often used when dealing with consent issues. 'Patient choice' in the context of consent is commonly misunderstood by health professionals and can be confused with a patient's rights under the Human Rights Act.[1]

'Patient choice' means that the patient may choose from the range of options offered to them. It does not mean that a patient can demand a particular course of treatment.

When managing patient care, a health professional assesses the patient and decides on the treatment and care. There may be several different options, including no treatment at all. Once the health professional has determined the options they are then offered to the patient. The patient can then choose from those options.

It must be appreciated that a patient has the right to determine what happens to their own body, they can accept or refuse treatment offered. Remember the fact that the patient has attended the hospital or an appointment is not implied consent to treatment. Think of it as a menu in a restaurant.

> When we go to a restaurant it may be implied that we are hungry so the chef says 'I have some lovely fish for you today, caught fresh this morning and prepared in coriander and garlic, it's delicious, you'll love it, you must have it'.
>
> Well maybe we are not that hungry, maybe we just wanted a cup of tea. 'No thanks, I don't want fish I am vegetarian and further I don't like coriander, I just want a cup of tea'. The chef is insistent, 'But you have come into my restaurant, therefore you must be very hungry, I got up early and caught it fresh, and I've spent a long time preparing it. It's good for you, so I'll give it to you anyway and you must eat it'.

When we go into a restaurant we expect to be presented with a menu of choices. In the same way a patient must be given the treatment options.

We explore the menu and may ask which options are vegetarian, or what the ingredients are. The chef may make recommendations. We then choose from the menu. Likewise, the health professional should provide the information in order for the patient to weigh up the options and choose.

If we go to a vegetarian restaurant we would not expect the chef to rustle up a steak for us that is not on the menu. In the same way a patient cannot demand treatment that health professionals do not consider to be clinically appropriate. Neither would we expect the chef to present us with the meal he would choose rather than the meal we would like. Health professionals should not impose treatment on a patient that is influenced by their own value judgments. It is up to the patient what they choose once they are given the choices.

Turning up at a restaurant does not imply that you are hungry or that you will eat anything that is presented to you. In the same way the fact that the patient has attended for an appointment does not imply that you can simply treat them as you wish.

Sometimes there may be options available for the patient but they are not available at that hospital or the PCT, such as expensive cancer drugs. But like in the restaurant we would say to the patient sorry we are vegetarian we don't serve steak.

The patient can be informed about the other options and how to access them such as seeking private care or making a payment to top up the costs, known as a copayment. However, there is still much controversy surrounding the issue where a patient is informed that they can make a copayment and can then have treatment that will extend their life. But having informed the patient, they may not be able to afford to make such copayment. This leaves the patient often upset and frustrated.

What happens if the patient wants only some of the choice?

EXAMPLE

The patient is offered choices of say:

1 A and B together – A, an operation followed by B, medication
2 C, different medication or
3 no treatment.

The patient says they want B but not A and refuses every other option.

If medication B is only appropriate following the operation and would have no benefit without the operation then the health professional can refuse to give only half of option 1 as it is no longer appropriate. The health professional should explain why this is so and offer them the alternative choices. It may be necessary to review the planned care and treatment options in order to do so.

Patient choice should not be confused with the patient's rights under the Human Rights Act 1998. Article 3 of the European Convention of Human Rights (ECHR)[2] confers the right of 'prohibition of torture, inhuman or degrading treatment or punishment'. This has the effect that the patient is entitled to medical treatment that should not breach this. Leaving a patient on a trolley in a corridor may be deemed degrading treatment and could be a breach of Article 3.[3] This is a human rights issue. The Human Rights Act does not confer a right allowing a patient to demand a particular course of treatment.

If the patient asks for a treatment that the doctor considers would not be of overall benefit to them, the doctor should discuss the issues with the patient and explore the reasons for their request. If, after discussion, the doctor still considers that the treatment would not be of overall benefit to the patient, they do not have to provide the treatment. But they should explain their reasons to the patient, and explain any other options that are available, including the option to seek a second opinion.[4]

It is important to remember that the health professional must provide the patient with the information they require in order that they may make decisions about their treatment. This includes options open to them. The patient should not be left wondering what options are available or take a chance and hope that they will like what they receive.

REFERENCES

1 Human Rights Act 1998
2 European Convention of Human Rights
3 European Convention of Human Rights Article 3
4 General Medical Council (GMC). *Consent: patients and doctors making decisions together.* London: General Medical Council; 2008. Pt 1 and p. 5(d).

CHAPTER 6

Refusing and withdrawing treatment

Before reading this chapter consider the scenario below.

Scenario

> Susan requires a caesarean section as the baby is in distress. Susan is refusing.
> If she does not have the treatment both she and the baby will die.
>> Can her refusal be overridden to save her life?
>> Can her refusal be overridden to save the unborn baby?

REFUSING TREATMENT

It is a basic principal of consent that a competent adult has the absolute right to consent to treatment or to refuse treatment. It does not matter whether the decision to refuse treatment is rational, irrational or for no reason at all. It is up to the patient even if the refusal results in her own death or that of her unborn child.[1]

Logically, there can be no difference between an ability to consent and an ability to refuse treatment. However, while consent involves acceptance of an experienced and professional view, refusal rejects that experience and professionalism and may do so from a position of limited understanding. Furthermore, a refusal of treatment may close down an option, which may be regretted later in life.[2]

As part of providing information to a patient, one of the options should be the patient's right to refuse treatment. Where a patient refuses treatment the patient should be informed of the consequences of refusing. The health professional should respect the patient's wishes to refuse treatment even if their decision is considered by the health professional to be wrong or irrational. The health professional should explain their concerns clearly to the patient and outline the possible consequences of their decision. The health professional must not, however, put pressure on a patient to accept their advice. If the health professional is unsure about the patient's capacity to make a decision, the health professional must follow the guidance under the Mental Capacity Act discussed in Chapter 17.

Where a competent adult makes a voluntary and informed decision to refuse treatment it must be respected. The courts have emphasised the importance of ensuring that when a patient refuses treatment, the patient has not been subject to adverse influence by another. It should be noted that presence of a mental disorder does not automatically mean that a person is incapable of making a valid decision in relation to treatment.

When a patient refuses treatment, there is an inherent conflict of interest for health professionals. It is very difficult to stand back and watch a patient deteriorate or die because they do not want to be treated. This can be very upsetting for health professionals. There is quite naturally a tendency to ignore the patient's refusal and to ask someone else to consent on their behalf, a spouse, or other family member, the doctor, a psychiatrist or even the cleaner as a last resort! Remember that no one else can consent on behalf of a competent adult, so to obtain consent from someone else would not be valid.

The patient will have their own reasons for refusing treatment and the health professional must not impose their own value judgment upon them. Health professionals should, however, still work in partnership with patient. It would be good practice to try to establish the patient's reasons or concerns for refusing treatment.

EXAMPLE

The patient may refuse treatment for terminal cancer. Their reason may be because their father died of cancer and the treatment was painful, the side-effects were unpleasant and he did not have a good quality of life. The patient does not want to go the same way.

However, it may be that the patient does not have the same cancer as his father, or his prognosis is better, or the treatment has changed. Explaining this to the patient may help them to reach the right decision for them.

The patient may not wish to say what the reasons for refusing treatment are. That is up to the patient and must be respected.

There is a tendency to presume that the patient who refuses treatment, which will result in their death or serious deterioration, must be irrational and therefore they lack capacity, as surely no right-minded person would refuse such treatment. However, regardless of whether the treatment is life saving or not, the same rules apply. Remember the basic principles, it is up to the patient, whether their decision is rational, irrational or for no reason at all. It must never be presumed that because a patient is refusing treatment they lack capacity. If there is any doubt about their capacity then the process under the Mental Capacity Act[3] must be applied. Lack of capacity must not be confused with an irrational decision.

Refusal: distinguishing capacity from an irrational decision.

THE CASE OF RE MB

MB required a caesarean section but refused to have the needle require for sedation on the basis that she had a needle phobia. The hospital requested a judicial declaration from the court to lawfully carry out the procedure.

It was established that at the time the decision had been made by MB her phobia impaired her capacity to take in the information about her condition and the proposed treatment.

The judge declared the treatment could lawfully proceed.

A phobia would be considered differently to an irrational decision. If, for example, MB had said 'I understand the procedure and I understand that if I do not have the procedure I will die and my baby will die, but I do not want to proceed because I do not believe in medical intervention in childbirth'. This may be considered irrational but not necessarily lacking capacity.

Would the judicial decision have been different if MB had not given a reason for her refusal? The answer is probably yes.

The courts have emphasised the importance of ensuring that when a patient refuses treatment they have not been subject to adverse influence by another.

Refusal and distinguishing capacity from a mental health condition

The presence of a mental disorder does not mean that a person is incapable of making a valid decision in relation to refusal of treatment.

CASE OF RE C

The patient was a 68-year-old man who suffered from paranoid schizophrenia and was detained at Broadmoor hospital. He developed gangrene in one foot. The doctors considered it was in the patient's best interest to amputate his foot to save his life. The patient refused to give consent. The patient had good periods where he was lucid and sometimes bad periods where his illness rendered him lacking capacity. He was concerned that when he went through a period where he lacked capacity the doctors would at that point undertake the amputation. The patient therefore sought an injunction restraining the hospital from carrying out the amputation should he lack capacity in the future.[4]

The issue considered by the court was whether he had capacity to give valid refusal. The court determined the case and on hearing the patient concluded that at the time the decision was made, the patient had:

➤ understood and retained the relevant treatment information
➤ believed it and
➤ weighed the balance to arrive at a clear choice.

The patient therefore had a right to refuse treatment but it must be clear that he was mentally competent at the time the decision is made.

This case was determined prior to the Mental Capacity Act (MCA).[5]

The distinguishing factor between capacity and irrational decision or psychiatric condition rendering the patient lacking capacity is the perception of reality.

For example, an adult patient suffering from anorexia may refuse treatment. If they refuse because notwithstanding they are grossly underweight, they believe they are too fat. This perception is not reality it is part of the condition. Whereas, if the patient said I realise if I do not eat it I will get even thinner and will probably die but I understand that, then that may be irrational but may not render them lacking capacity and their refusal should be respected.

Capacity is discussed in detail in Chapter 17.

REFUSAL AND ACTING IN AN EMERGENCY

Where a patient refuses life-saving treatment health professionals cannot impose treatment under the guise of acting in an emergency to save the patient's life. Where the adult patient is competent their wishes must be respected.

This is not the same as acting in an emergency to save life where the patient cannot give or refuse consent because they are unconscious or lack capacity for some other reason.

IMPACT ON RESOURCES

Where a patient refuses treatment the health professional cannot impose treatment because of the cost implications.

EXAMPLE

A patient is diagnosed with diabetes but is refusing insulin treatment which is required. Such refusal will result in additional costs as the patient will deteriorate and will require more frequent home visits and greater degree of palliative care.

While this will undoubtedly impact on resources it cannot be the reason for ignoring the patient's refusal.

MANAGING THE PATIENT WHO REFUSES TREATMENT

Where a patient refuses a particular intervention, the health professionals must ensure that they continue to provide any other appropriate care to which the patient has consented. The health professional should also ensure that the patient knows that they are free to change their mind and accept treatment later if they wish.

Where a delay may affect their treatment choices, the patient should be advised accordingly.

Where treatment is refused it is essential to take all reasonable precautions to ensure that the patient has been appropriately counselled and given all relevant information and help facing the future.

The health professionals should do what they can to make the patient as comfortable as possible.

If a patient consents to a particular procedure but refuses certain aspects of their care, the health professional must explain to the patient the possible consequences of their partial refusal.

If the health professional genuinely believes that the care cannot be safely carried out under the patient's stipulated conditions, health professionals are not obliged to undertake the procedure. However, the health professional must continue to provide any other appropriate care. It may be necessary to review the planned care and treatment options and to obtain consent for those alternative options in the usual way.

Where a patient refuses treatment, this should be clearly documented in their notes.

There are exceptions to refusal of treatment where minors and those detained under the Mental Health Act 1983[6] are concerned. These are dealt with later in Chapter 17.

Own discharge

It follows that as a patient has the right to accept or refuse treatment they also have the corresponding right to discharge themselves, even against medical advice.

Where a patient discharges themselves health professionals should make a good record in the notes of the advice given and any other relevant circumstances.

Patients who discharge themselves can be a concern for health professionals. A patient who presents with a head injury but refuses treatment and wishes to discharge himself must be handled with great care. It could be the case that the patient lacks capacity due to a head injury and his life may be in danger if he discharges himself. In these circumstances the health professional may be justified in preventing the patient from leaving to save his life in an emergency. The health professional must do a proper assessment of capacity and this must be well documented in the notes.

If the patient is competent he must be allowed to leave. The patient should sign a self-discharge form and if this is not possible the health professional must make a full record of the circumstances leading to self-discharge and the efforts made to encourage the patient to stay.

Advance refusal of consent is discussed in Chapter 18.

WITHDRAWAL OF CONSENT

A patient who has consented to treatment is entitled to withdraw their consent at any time. Withdrawal of consent must not prejudice the patient's care.

The health professional must give the patient the opportunity to withdraw consent.

This may take the form of initially informing the patient they can withdraw their consent at any time. During the ongoing consent process it is not necessary to expressly state each time that they can withdraw consent but may say, for example, 'today I am going to take blood, are you happy for me to continue or do you have any questions?' This will give the patient the opportunity to withdraw consent. If there is any doubt about the patient's consent it is advisable to be more explicit regarding their right to withdraw it.

Where a patient withdraws consent, this should be clearly documented in their notes. If the patient has signed a consent form and then changes their mind, and withdraws consent the health professional, and ideally the patient, should record this on the consent form.

Withdrawing consent during a procedure

A patient has the right to withdraw consent at any time even during the performance of a procedure.

EXAMPLE

A patient is undergoing an endoscopy without anaesthetic. The patient cries out 'ouch, that hurts'.

Is this a withdrawal of consent?

Where a patient objects during treatment, it is good practice for the health professional, if at all possible, to stop the procedure, establish the patient's concerns, and explain the consequences of not completing the procedure.

Sometimes an apparent objection may reflect a cry of pain rather than withdrawal of consent, and appropriate reassurance may enable the practitioner to continue with the patient's consent. If stopping the procedure at that point would genuinely put the life of the patient at risk, the practitioner may be entitled to continue until the risk no longer applies.

Assessing capacity during a procedure may be difficult and, factors such as pain, panic and shock may diminish capacity to consent. The practitioner should try to establish whether at that time the patient has capacity to withdraw a previously given consent. If the patient does not have capacity, it may some-times be justified to continue in the patient's best interests although this should not be used as an excuse to ignore distress.

REFERENCES

1 Re MB (Adult, medical treatment) [1997] 38 BMLR 175 CA
2 Mason and McCall 1994
3 Mental Capacity Act 2005
4 Re C (Adult: Refusal of Treatment) [1994] 1 WLR 290; [1994] 1 All ER 819
5 Mental Capacity Act 2005
6 Mental Health Act 1983

CHAPTER 7

Relatives' rights

Under English law, no one is able to give consent to the examination or treatment of an adult unable to give consent for him or herself (an 'incapable' adult). Therefore, parents, relatives or members of the healthcare team cannot consent on behalf of such an adult.

There is little point in asking a spouse, parent or sibling, for example, to sign a consent form as this has no legal status and does not constitute valid consent. Remember the basic principle is that a patient has a right to accept or refuse treatment whether it is rational, irrational or for no reason at all even if it results in their own death. No one, not even next of kin can consent on behalf of a competent adult.

It is not uncommon for health professionals to seek information from family members. In these circumstances the health professional is not obtaining consent from the family they are merely gathering information in order to determine what is in the best interests of the patient. Remember though that in discussing information with the family, the health professional could be in breach of patient confidentiality.

In practice health professionals are sometimes faced with difficult situations.

EXAMPLE

A 24-year-old mentally competent male has refused treatment for a blood transfusion following a road traffic accident. The health professionals believe it is in the patient's best interest to receive blood. Without it he will die. The mother is beside herself with fear that her son will die. The health profession-als have difficulty standing back and watching him die. There is a temptation for the health professionals to ask the parents to consent to treatment on the young man's behalf. They also fear that the mother will sue the hospital if they don't save him.

In practice, it is very difficult to stand back and watch a patient die. However, in these circumstances consent cannot be obtained from the family and the health professionals cannot override the wishes of the patient.

I am sure those reading this are now desperately searching for another way of being able to proceed to giving this patient the blood transfusion. Ask the consultant to consent on the patient's behalf. Ask the family to consent. Question the patient's capacity due to pain or because it's an irrational deci-sion. Get the psychiatrist to say he lacks capacity. Ask the cleaner! Anyone, as long as we can carry out the treatment.

Notwithstanding this difficult situation, to proceed with treatment with-out consent is unlawful.

In practice, this should be dealt with by working in partnership with the patient. Ensuring the patient has received all of the information, has under-stood it and the consequences of refusing it. If the patient refuses treatment this must be respected.

Relatives do not have the right to consent to treatment on behalf of a competent adult.

CHAPTER 8

Forms of consent

Before reading this chapter consider the following questions:

Which form of consent has more weight in law: in writing, verbal or implied?

Does a signed consent form constitute valid consent?

Consent is a process of communication. The Kennedy Report[1] recommendations stated:

➤ The process of informing the patient, and obtaining consent to a course of treatment, should be regarded as a process and not a one-off event consisting of obtaining a patient's signature on a form.

➤ The process of consent should apply not only to surgical procedures but also to all clinical procedures and examinations that involve any form of touching. This does not mean more forms: it means more communication.

Consent may be given in different forms. It may be in writing, verbal or implied. As far as the law is concerned there is no specific requirement that consent for treatment should be given in any particular way. They are all equally valid.

They do, however, vary in their value as evidence in proving consent was given.

IN WRITING

Completion of a consent form in the majority of cases is not a legal requirement. Except by law you must get written consent for certain treatments, for example, under the Mental Health Act 1983[2] and the Human Fertilisation and Embryology Act 1990.[3] You must follow the laws and codes of practice that govern these situations.

For most situations, however, there is no requirement for consent to be in writing. However, consent in writing is by far the best form of evidence that valid consent was obtained. It is therefore the preferred method of obtaining consent of the patient.

While it may not be appropriate to obtain consent in writing in every situation it is obtained usually when any procedure involving risk is contemplated, where the treatment is complex or perhaps where the procedure is invasive.

You should consider obtaining consent in writing where:

➤ the investigation or treatment is complex or involves significant risks
➤ there may be significant consequences for the patient's employment, or social or personal life
➤ providing clinical care is not the primary purpose of the investigation or treatment
➤ the treatment is part of a research programme or is an innovative treatment designed specifically for the patient's benefit.

Written consent serves as evidence. However, if the elements of voluntariness, appropriate information and capacity have not been satisfied, a signature on a consent form will not make the consent valid.

Where there is any doubt about the patient's capacity, it is important, before the patient is asked to sign the form, to establish both that they have the capacity to consent to the intervention and that they have received enough information to enable valid consent to be given. Details of the assessment of capacity, and the conclusion reached, should be recorded in the notes.

Consent forms

A signature on a consent form does not in itself constitute valid consent. Consent is a process of communication. The details of the agreed procedure and risks, etc., are then recorded on a form, which may then be signed by the patient as evidence that the patient agrees.

The Department of Health (DH) provides advice and model forms of consent. Often forms are developed at a local level to cover certain procedures. These can be useful but health professionals must be cautious of issues that are not included in these standard forms, for example, risks relating to pre-existing conditions.

The consent forms may consist of tick boxes. A tick box may read, 'has the patient been advised of the risks?' This tick box lacks the detail required.

It is now more common on standard forms to see the words, 'I confirm the patient has been advised of the following risks . . .' The detailed advice given in respect of the risks is then clearly recorded.

To say, 'the reason why I did not record detail was that there was no room on the form', is not a defence. If there is no room on the form the detail should be written in the records.

When using consent forms the health professional must ensure that the relevant consent to carry out the procedure has been obtained.

For example, a consent form commonly used in the NHS that gives a surgeon the right to carry out an operation also gives the right to undertake '. . . any other procedures that are deemed necessary'. However, unless these additional procedures are related to the operation for which consent has been expressly given, or can be justified out of necessity they will not be covered by such consent.

EXAMPLE

A patient has a history of uterine bleeding and is to undergo a laparoscopy. The patient is advised of the risks of the laparoscopy and signs the consent form. The consent form includes 'and any other procedure deemed necessary'. During the procedure the surgeon discovers a polyp which he removes for biopsy and suspects this polyp is the cause of the bleeding.

The removal of the polyp results in excessive bleeding, leading to infection.

Was valid consent obtained?

The answer is no. The patient consented to the laparoscopy but not to the removal of the polyp. It must be clear what procedures are being carried out and to advise the patient of the risks associated with it. Without valid consent to remove the polyp the surgeon should in these circumstances let the patient recover from the anaesthetic explain they found the polyp and arrange for the patient to undergo a further procedure. They cannot proceed to operate for the convenience of the surgeon or because of the financial costs of rearranging it.

The best procedure is to anticipate in advance whether any further procedure is likely to be necessary and obtain consent beforehand, having given the patient all of the information and risks relating to it.

From the court's point of view the fact that the patient has signed the consent form and therefore expressly agreed that the nature and extent of the operation has been explained, would be strong evidence to defend any action for trespass to the person.

However, there is a possibility that a claim may be successful in an action for negligence, if the patient has not been given relevant information.

There is a clear duty on the doctor to take all reasonable care that a patient receives the appropriate information before any consent form is signed and treatment proceeds.

The healthcare professional has a legal duty to the patient and if he knows that the patient has not understood what they have signed or failed to take in the information, the health professional should arrange for the explanation to be given again.

A nurse who is aware that a patient has not understood should take appropriate steps to inform the doctor.

Signing the consent form

When dealing with adults only the patient should sign the consent form. No one else should sign it. The consent form should never be signed by anyone else, such as a spouse, parent, sibling, relative or health professional, on the patients behalf.

This is different to the position where a doctor signs a consent form regarding a termination for pregnancy. They are not signing to consent for treatment on behalf of a patient, they are signing that they have complied with the legality regarding termination.

If the patient has capacity, but is illiterate, the patient may be able to make their mark on the form to indicate consent. It would be good practice for the mark to be witnessed by a person other than the health professional seeking consent, and for the fact that the patient has chosen to make their mark in this way to be recorded in the case notes. Similarly, if the patient has capacity, and wishes to give consent, but is physically unable to mark the form, this fact should be recorded in the notes. If consent has been validly given, the lack of a completed form is no bar to treatment.

When dealing with children someone with parental responsibility may sign the consent form.

VERBAL CONSENT

Many less risky procedures are carried out without any formal signature of the patient. Verbal consent is valid but it is difficult to establish in court as it is one person's word against another.

Many day-to-day treatments are carried out on the basis of verbal consent. It would be prudent for health professionals to make a record of verbal consent in the notes where appropriate.

EXAMPLE

A care plan was agreed to by the patient. An entry in the records should confirm that the care plan was discussed and agreed and verbal consent was obtained.

IMPLIED CONSENT

It is often said that when a patient comes into hospital it means that they are consenting to treatment. That, however, is not supported by the law. This does not constitute implied consent.

Similarly, it is often said that when an unconscious patient is treated in the emergency department, the fact they are unconscious implies consent to being treated. This is not supported by the law. An unconscious patient implies nothing. Health professionals care for the unconscious patient in the absence of consent as part of their duty of care to the patient out of necessity in an emergency to save life and may be able to defend any action against them on that basis.

There are many choices of available treatment and when care is provided there must be evidence that the patient has agreed to that particular course of treatment.

Implied consent is where non-verbal communication by the patient makes it clear that consent is given. For example, after receiving appropriate information, a patient rolls up their sleeve and holds out an arm for their blood pressure to be taken, or the patient opens their mouth as the nurse waves the thermometer in the air.

Such actions indicate to the nurse that the patient agrees to the treatment proceeding.

No words are spoken there is no signature but it is clear that the patient is in agreement.

The weakness of implied consent is that it is not always clear what the nurse intended to do. For example, the patient who rolls up his sleeve for blood pressure to be taken would get a nasty shock if the nurse gave him an injection.

To avoid such misunderstanding it is preferable for the nurse to tell the patient what she wishes to do and to obtain verbal consent from the patient.

Consequences

Once a mentally competent patient has given valid consent to treatment then the patient cannot succeed in an action for trespass to the person.

However, if it is claimed that insufficient information was given or the risks were not explained, the patient may bring an action in negligence alleging breach of duty of care in failing to provide sufficient information.

REFERENCES

1 Kennedy Report, July 2001, recommendations 24, 25
2 Mental Health Act 1983
3 Human Fertilisation and Embryology Act 1990

CHAPTER 9

Informed consent

What is informed consent?

How much information should be given to a patient?

HOW MUCH INFORMATION SHOULD BE GIVEN?

Before treatment can commence a patient must be given sufficient information in a way that they can understand what is proposed, possible alternatives and any material or significant risks relevant to that patient in his or her particular circumstances, so that they can make a balanced judgment in reaching a decision on whether to give or withhold consent. The information should also include no treatment at all and the consequences of not receiving it. Where relevant, information about anaesthesia should be given as well as information about the procedure itself.

The GMC states:

> In deciding how much information to share with your patients you should take account of their wishes. The information you share should be in proportion to the nature of their condition, the complexity of the proposed investigation or treatment, and the seriousness of any potential side-effects, complications or other risks.
>
> Serious or persistent failure to follow this guidance will put your registration at risk. You must, therefore, be prepared to explain and justify your actions.[1]

In order for consent to be valid the patient needs to understand in broad terms the nature and purpose of the procedure and the risks associated with it. Any misrepresentation of these elements may invalidate consent.

In the USA, when informing the patient they are usually handed a 50-page-or-so document covering every eventuality. In England and Wales we do not present such a document and a health professional is not required to inform the patient of absolutely everything but they will explain the usual half a dozen or so risks and sometimes also give them a leaflet to take away to read.

Where valid consent is obtained the patient cannot later claim trespass or that a battery occurred. Consent is a defence to a civil claim for trespass and to a charge of battery. However, if sufficient information is not given to the patient this may constitute a breach of duty of care and the patient may make a civil claim for compensation, if they were injured as a result.

EXAMPLE

Julie is informed about the proposed laparoscopic cholecystectomy to remove her gallstones. She is told about the procedure, the alternatives of open surgery or conservative treatment including medication to dissolve the gallstones, and an ultrasound. She is informed of the risks of excessive bleeding or developing a blood clot in a vein in the leg (deep vein thrombosis, DVT). Julie chooses the laparoscopic procedure and signs the consent form.

Julie had not been informed about the risks of infection. Neither was she informed about the risk of a reaction to the anaesthetic.

Following the procedure Julie developed an infection at the entry site of the laparoscopy and is seriously ill requiring IV antibiotics. Her recovery is delayed and she is left with significant scarring around the wound site. Julie states she was not informed about the risk of infection and had she been told she would not have had the procedure.

Complaints in relation to consent often include a failure to inform the patient of the risks. Even where a consent form is signed this does not constitute valid consent unless all of the elements of valid consent have been adhered to.

***So how much information should the patient be given? Do they need to
know every possible risk?***

There is no clear right in law for the patient to insist on being told everything
even where he is exercising his right under the Data Protections Act.

Sidaway case

The requirements of the legal duty to inform patients have been significantly
developed in case law during the last decade. In 1985, the House of Lords
decided in the Sidaway[2] case that the legal standard to be used when deciding whether adequate information had been given to a patient should be the
same as that used when judging whether a doctor had been negligent in their
treatment or care of a patient. A doctor would not be considered negligent
if their practice conformed to that of a responsible body of medical opinion
held by practitioners skilled in the field in question (known as the 'Bolam
test').[3] Whether the duty of care had been satisfied was therefore primarily
a matter of medical opinion.

This has the effect that the amount of information that must be given to
a patient is based on whether a responsible body of practitioners would have
given that information.

However, the Sidaway case also stated that it was open to the courts to
decide that information about a particular risk was so obviously necessary
that it would be negligent not to provide it, even if a 'responsible body' of
medical opinion would not have done so.

Since Sidaway, judgments in a number of negligence cases (relating both
to the provision of information and to the standard of treatment given) have
shown that courts are willing to be critical of a 'responsible body' of medical opinion. It is now clear that the courts will be the final arbiter of what
constitutes responsible practice, although the standards set by the health
professions for their members will still be influential.

The exchange of information between the health professional and
the patient is central to good decision-making. How much information
the health professional shares with patients will vary, depending on their
individual circumstances. The approach should be tailored taking into consideration the following:

➤ their needs, wishes and priorities
➤ their level of knowledge about, and understanding of, their condition,
  prognosis and the treatment options
➤ the nature of their condition

> the complexity of the treatment, and
> the nature and level of risk associated with the investigation or
   treatment.

You should not make assumptions about the information a patient might want
or need, the clinical or other factors a patient might consider significant, or
a patient's level of knowledge or understanding of what is proposed.

The health professional must never impose their own value judgments.
This can be particularly testing when the patient is refusing treatment.

The health professional must give patients the information they want or
need about:

> the diagnosis and prognosis
> any uncertainties about the diagnosis or prognosis, including options for
   further investigations
> options for treating or managing the condition, including the option
   not to treat
> the purpose of any proposed investigation or treatment and what it will
   involve, the potential benefits, risks and burdens, and the likelihood of
   success, for each option; this should include information, if available,
   about whether the benefits or risks are affected by which organisation or
   doctor is chosen to provide care
> whether a proposed investigation or treatment is part of a research
   programme or is an innovative treatment designed specifically for their
   benefit
> the people who will be mainly responsible for and involved in their
   care, what their roles are, and to what extent students may be involved
> their right to refuse to take part in teaching or research
> their right to seek a second opinion
> any fees they will have to pay
> any conflicts of interest that you, or your organisation, may have
> any treatments that you believe have greater potential benefit for the
   patient than those you or your organisation can offer.

Explaining the risks
In order to have effective discussions with patients about risk, the health
professional must identify the adverse outcomes that may result from the
proposed options.

This includes the potential outcome of taking no action. Risks can take a number of forms, such as side-effects, complications or failure of an intervention to achieve the desired aim. Risks can vary from common but minor side-effects, to rare but serious adverse outcomes possibly resulting in permanent disability or death.

In assessing the risk to an individual patient, the health professional must consider the nature of the patient's condition, their general health and other circumstances.

These are variable factors that may affect the likelihood of adverse outcomes occurring. The health professional should do their best to understand the patient's views and preferences about any proposed investigation or treatment, and the adverse outcomes they are most concerned about.

Birch v University College London 2008

The patient was admitted to hospital. An MRI scan was recommended by the consultant to exclude the possibility that she was suffering from an aneurism or cavernous sinus pathology. No MRI slots were available at the hospital so the patient was transferred to neurosurgical ward where an invasive catheter angiography was performed. This had increased risks to patients with her condition. The associated risks of angiography were explained to the patient and she then signed the consent form. Subsequently, there were complications with the angiography and it resulted in a stroke. The effect of the stroke on the patient's life was traumatic, she was left disabled.

The court concluded if there was a significant risk that would affect the judgment of a reasonable patient then, in the normal circumstances, it was the responsibility of a doctor to inform the patient of that risk so as to enable him to determine for himself which course he should adopt. The duty to inform a patient of significant risks would not be discharged unless and until a patient was made aware that fewer or no risks were associated with another available and alternative treatment.[4]

Thus the duty to inform a patient of the significant risks of a medical procedure was only discharged if the patient was made aware of the alternative procedure (if any) with fewer or no risks associated. The patient should therefore have been told that an alternative procedure (MRI) with fewer risks was available.

The health professional must therefore explain to the patient the alternative options with the associated risks of each option.

Chester v Asfar

Small but significant risk

This case involved a patient who underwent surgery on the spinal column. There was a small but unavoidable risk (1–2%) that the proposed operation, however expertly performed, might lead to a seriously adverse result, known as cauda equina syndrome. The doctor advised the patient of some of the risks but did not advise her of the small risk of cauda equina damage occurring.

The patient did suffer cauda equina resulting in her being severely disabled. The patient said that if she had been warned of the risk she would not have agreed to surgery and would have minimised the risk of surgery by entrusting herself to a different surgeon, or undergoing a different form of surgery.

The court concluded that the patient was not informed of this risk and because of the risk of significant harm, she should have been told.[5]

Thus even if there is a small risk which may result in significant harm, the patient should be told. This is why it is now routine to inform patients of the risk of death under anesthetic.

In practice, there are usually half a dozen or so risk factors that are discussed with the patient. There is an abundance of information that may be necessary to inform the patient too many to list here but the kind of information that is likely to be given to the patient may include:

➤ the main treatment options
➤ the purpose and detail of the treatment options
➤ the benefits of each of the options
➤ the risks, if any, of each option, including all serious risks, however unlikely to occur, and all commonly occurring risks
➤ side-effects
➤ the success rates for the different options – nationally, for the unit or for the health professional or surgeon
➤ name of the doctor with overall responsibility
➤ why the suggested treatment is necessary
➤ prognosis
➤ the risks of not having treatment
➤ reminder that the patient can change their mind at any time.

The health professionals must give information about risk in a balanced way. They should avoid bias, and they should explain the expected benefits as well as the potential burdens and risks of any proposed investigation or treatment.

Remember to bear in mind that even the smallest risks can be matters that may be a cause of concern to the patient. You must inform them, for example, the medication may make the patients urine turn blue and that it is nothing to worry about. Otherwise the patient may panic when they see blue urine and may wonder what's happening to them.

The health professional must use clear, simple and consistent language when discussing risks with patients. Be aware that patients may understand information about risk differently from the health professional. Check that the patient understands the terms that are used, particularly when describing the seriousness, frequency and likelihood of an adverse outcome. Use simple and accurate written information or visual or other aids to explain risk, if they will help the patient to understand.

Remember to have regard to the patient's values and beliefs. For example, when advising on risks of medication it may be appropriate to mention that the medication contains animal fat. This may be extremely important to vegetarians or some religious sectors when making their choice.

When providing information to a patient a health professional must not impose their own value judgments. The health professional must always act in the best interest of the patient. Remember the basic principle: it is the patients' right to determine what happens to them. Sometimes there can be an inherent conflict where the patient does not wish to accept the option that is preferred by the health professional. Where a health professional imposes their own values on a patient they are in danger of invalidating consent and will be accountable.

Extra information

A health professional is not required to inform the patient of absolutely everything. Remember they must be given sufficient information in order for them to make a balanced decision. However, where the patient requests further or specific questions about the procedure and associated risks these should be answered truthfully.

The obligation of the health professional is to provide sufficient information so the patient can reach a decision, as set out above. If the patient wishes to know more, it is for the patient to ask for it.

Patients may wish to ask questions about the treatment itself or questions about how the treatment might affect their future health or lifestyle, for example:

➤ when are they likely to be able to return to work

➤ whether they will need long-term care
➤ will their mobility be affected
➤ will they still be able to drive
➤ will it affect the kind of work they do
➤ will it affect their personal/sexual relationships
➤ will they be able to take part in their favourite sport/exercises or hobbies
➤ will they have to change their diet.

You must answer patients' questions honestly and, as far as practical, answer as fully as they wish.

WHAT IF THE PATIENT DOES NOT WANT TO BE TOLD?

Some patients may wish to know very little about the treatment which is being proposed. If information is offered and declined, this fact should be recorded in the notes. However, it is possible that patients' wishes may change over time, and it is important to provide opportunities for them to express this.

Where a patient declines to be informed this does not prevent the health professional from proceeding with the treatment. It is good practice to explain to patients the importance of knowing the options open to them. The health professional should try to find out why they do not want the information. Basic information should always be provided.

If, after discussion, a patient still does not want to know in detail about their condition or the treatment, you should respect their wishes, as far as possible. But you must still give them the information they need in order to give their consent to a proposed investigation or treatment. This is likely to include what the investigation or treatment aims to achieve and what it will involve, for example: whether the procedure is invasive, what level of pain or discomfort they might experience, and what can be done to minimise it; anything they should do to prepare for the investigation or treatment; and if it involves any serious risks.

If a patient insists that they do not want even this basic information, you must explain the potential consequences of them not having it, particularly if it might mean that their consent is not valid. You must record the fact that the patient has declined this information. You must also make it clear that they can change their mind and have more information at any time.

CAN INFORMATION BE WITHHELD?

In the very rare event that the health professional believes that to fully inform the patient would cause serious harm and have a deleterious effect on the patient's health, the information can be withheld. This view, and the reasons for it, should be recorded in the patient's notes. When such concerns arise it is advisable to discuss the issue within the team caring for the patient. In an individual case the courts may accept such a justification but would examine it with great care.

A health professional cannot withhold information about risks because he believes the patient would not consent to it. The mere fact that the patient might become upset by hearing the information is not sufficient to act as a justification. There must be other reasons to justify withholding this information. The health professional must show that there is a significant risk of harm if the patient is told.

Information should not be withheld because relatives, partners or friends of the patient have asked you to. It is often the case that the relatives cannot deal with the situation and is requested when a patient has a diagnosis of terminal illness or poor prognosis. It is difficult for the relatives to deal with this situation. A request from the family is insufficient justification for withholding information. The decision to withhold information must only be exercised where there is evidence that it will cause harm to the patient. Remember the duty of care is to the patient. To withhold information may be a breach of that duty. The patient is entitled to have this information remain confidential. Withholding information from the patient but discussing the matter with relatives may be a breach of confidentiality.

The health professional should regularly review their decision to withhold information, and consider whether they could give information to the patient later, without causing them serious harm.

THERAPEUTIC PRIVILEGE

If a patient is terminally ill, should the nurse tell the patient contrary to medical advice?

What will the nurse do if the patient asks, 'do I have cancer?' or, 'is it worth me booking a holiday next year?'

The nurse should withhold information if it is deemed to be in the interest of the patient. This is known as 'therapeutic privilege'. Informing a patient that she is terminally ill may come under this heading. Where the decision to withhold information has been made by the doctor, the nurse should not take it upon herself to tell the patient. But the nurse should not lie to the patient. So, if the patient makes it clear that she is seeking further information then the nurse should take steps to arrange for the patient to speak to the doctor. The nurse should inform the doctor that the patient is asking such questions. The doctor may then review the decision as to whether they should continue to withhold the information.

EXAMPLE

What is the position if the relatives do not wish the patient to be told?

Although this is really an issue of confidentiality it may impact on consent in so far as the patient may not be fully informed.

A patient of 37 years is operated on for a polyp and the surgeon finds an inoperable tumor that has spread, and she has a life expectancy of three months. The doctor is normally in favour of openness, but considers in this case that the patient would not be able to cope with the information, and the patient's husband agrees.

The nursing staff are advised accordingly.

The consultant or GP has clinical responsibility for the patient so if they believe that the patient may be harmed by disclosure of information then the rest of the team must accept and implement the decision.

Any health professional that went against the doctor's advice and informed the patient may face disciplinary action.

HAS THE PATIENT UNDERSTOOD?

Sometimes it is difficult to determine if a patient has understood the information. Patients will often be passive and may not have the confidence to say they have failed to understand something. There may be many barriers such as language, hearing difficulties or illiteracy. Consider whether the patient needs any additional support to understand information, to communicate their wishes, or to make a decision. It may be necessary to have an interpreter present or to read out the leaflet to the patient. It may be necessary to support discussions by using written material, or visual or other aids. Make sure the material is accurate and up to date.

A good way of checking whether the patient has understood the information is to ask them to repeat it back to the health professional in their own words. This will give the health professional an indication as to whether they have understood.

LANGUAGE

The health professional must have regard to the patient's understanding, which can be hampered by, for example, language or literacy barriers.

If there is a language barrier, this should be clearly recorded. The health professional must ask themselves: does the patient require an interpreter?

If an interpreter is used, record their name and ask the interpreter to countersign the record as having correctly interpreted.

If a family member is being used to interpret, the health professional must be careful to use them appropriately and be aware of the confidentiality issues this raises. Health professionals must ask themselves: is it appropriate to have a family member as interpreter? Is there a risk of coercion? Failure to deal with these issues could invalidate consent and may also be a breach of confidentiality.

It should also be noted that there may be language barriers due to the health professionals having a strong accent, a weakness in English grammar, limited vocabulary or different mouth movements making lip reading difficult for those hard of hearing.

Where there are any issues regarding language and understanding, it is important to record the details.

LEAFLETS AND TAPE RECORDING

Where a leaflet is given to the patient, how does the health professional know they can read it? Is the patient literate? Patients who are illiterate are very clever at disguising it. They may not admit they are illiterate for fear of embarrassment.

Giving information via leaflets or tape recordings can be a good way of providing information. They should not, however, replace the need to discuss information with the patient face to face.

Leaflets are useful, as the patient can read and consider the information at their leisure, and they give them the opportunity for discussion with family. It is important to check that the leaflet is in their language so that they can understand it.

Tape recordings of a consultation are sometimes given to the patient. Again this is useful as it gives the patient the opportunity to consider it again and discuss it with family if they wish. It allows them to consider if there is anything they wish to ask.

A note that a particular leaflet or tape has been given to the patient should be recorded in the notes.

SHOULD THE PATIENT BE INFORMED WHERE PROCEDURES ARE CARRIED OUT BY STUDENTS OR TRAINEES?

Providing clear information is particularly important when students or trainees carry out procedures to further their own education. Where the procedure will further the patient's care, for example, taking a blood sample for testing, assuming the student is appropriately trained in the procedure, the fact that it is carried out by a student does not alter the nature and purpose of the procedure. It is therefore not a legal requirement to tell the patient that the health professional is a student, although it would always be good practice to do so. In contrast, where a student proposes to conduct a physical examination which is not part of the patient's care, then it is essential to explain that the purpose of the examination is to further the student's training and to seek consent for that to take place.

ADDITIONAL PROCEDURES

During an operation it may become evident that the patient could benefit from an additional procedure that was not within the scope of the original consent.

To avoid complications around consent it is good practice to plan ahead and consider whether there are any possible additional procedures when seeking consent to the original intervention and to obtain the consent of the patient to undertake them. It is not appropriate to simply obtain consent to 'any additional procedures that may be required'. This does not constitute valid consent. Remember the patient should be informed of the procedure and risks and so on, so that they can make a decision. The patient should be informed about the possible additional procedures.

The health professional should discuss with the patient the possibility of additional problems coming to light during an investigation or treatment when they might not be in a position to make a decision about how to proceed. If there is a significant risk of a particular problem arising, the patient should be asked in advance what they would like to do if it arises. The health professional should also ask if there are any procedures they object to, or which they would like more time to think about.

If during treatment it becomes apparent that the patient would benefit from an additional procedure, if consent has not been obtained the health professional should not proceed. The patient should be allowed to recover and any additional procedure carried out at a later time once consent has been obtained.

If during a procedure it would be unreasonable to delay it until the patient regains consciousness (for example, because there is a threat to the patient's life), it may be justifiable to perform the procedure on the grounds that it is in the patient's best interests. However, the procedure should not be performed merely because it is convenient. A hysterectomy should never be performed during an operation without explicit consent, unless it is necessary to do so to save life.

Where a patient has refused in advance regarding certain additional procedures before the anaesthetic (for example, specifying that a mastectomy should not be carried out after a frozen section biopsy result) this must be respected if the refusal is applicable to the circumstances.

INVOLVING FAMILIES, CARERS AND ADVOCATES

Health professionals should accommodate a patient's wishes if they want another person, such as a relative, partner, friend, carer or advocate, to be involved in discussions or to help them make decisions.

TIME RESTRAINTS

Health professionals can often be frustrated when the treatment or procedure takes five minutes but the consent process prior to the procedure takes half an hour. Not having enough time, or where the time it takes is, in the belief of the health professional, not justifiable, is no defence to treating a patient without consent. Regardless of lack of resources, the consent process must be adhered to otherwise there will no valid consent and the health professional will be accountable.

Where it is difficult, because of pressures on time or there are limited resources available to give patients the information or support needed to make decisions, the health professional should consider the role that other members of the healthcare team might play, and what other sources of information and support are available. This may include patient information leaflets, advocacy services, expert patient programmes, or support groups for people with specific conditions.

The health professional should do their best to make sure that patients with additional needs, such as those with disabilities, have the time and support they need to make a decision. Patients must be treated fairly and not be discriminated.

Where the health professional considers that limits on their ability to give patients the time or information they need is seriously compromising the patient's ability to make an informed decision, they should raise their concerns with their manager or employer.

REFERENCES

1 General Medical Council (GMC). *Consent: patients and doctors making decisions together.* London: General Medical Council; 2008. p. 5.
2 Sidaway v Bethlem Royal Hospital Governors [1985] AC 871
3 Bolam v Friern Barnet HMC [1957] 2 All ER 118
4 Birch v University College London Hospital NHS Foundation Trust [2008] EWHC 2237
5 Chester v Afshar [2004] UKHL 41; [2005] 1 AC 134; [2004] 3 WLR 927; [2004] 4 All ER 587

CHAPTER 10

Documenting consent

DOCUMENTING CONSENT ISSUES

When health professionals give advice and information to patients as part of the consent process it is important that it is well documented. This will ensure that everyone managing the patient is clear that the patient has consented to the treatment.

Records documenting consent should show that the health professional has discharged their duty of care. The records should demonstrate that they have properly informed the patient. The purpose of documenting the risks is to ensure that the patient has been fully advised so that they may make a decision regarding their care.

Some consent issues may be recorded on standard forms and others written in the health records. Not all consent issues will be written as some of them may be implied. Consent may have been given orally, if so, a clear record of this must be made.

The records may be used as evidence to show that valid consent was obtained. They will be used to answer any allegation in respect of a civil claim for damages for trespass to the person or a criminal charge of assault and battery.

When making a record, health professionals need to bear in mind the following points:

RECORDING RISKS

When advising the patient of the risks associated with treatment it is not sufficient simply to record in the notes 'patient advised of risks'. This does not provide enough information for other health professionals dealing with the care of the patient to ascertain precisely what was discussed. Details of the risks the health professional advised the patient must be recorded.

For example, the patient may have been informed of the known risks of a particular procedure but may not have been informed of the additional risks of a pre-existing underlying condition such as diabetes or a heart problem. If the entry in the record simply reads 'patient advised of risks', the health professionals involved in the patient care and treatment may make an assumption that the patient had been advised of all of those risks, when in fact the patient had not.

If a dispute arises regarding the risks that were advised the records will be relied upon in order to resolve the dispute. A patient may agree that risks were discussed but may say, 'yes, you advised me of the risks. However, you said I might get an infection but you did not tell me that I might bleed and had I known that I would not have had the operation'. This highlights one of the problems that can be faced by health professionals in failing to document consent issues fully.

The health professional will need to demonstrate with the aid of the records which risks they actually advised the patient.

Failing to record the details of the risks about which the patient has been advised could mislead other health professionals involved in the patient's care.

WHAT TO INCLUDE?

Health professionals must ensure that a good record is clearly set out in the notes. It should include the facts presented to the patient, information discussed, any specific requests made by the patient, any written, visual or audio information given to the patient, details of the decisions made. When giving the patient advice, health professionals should also include in the records the advice given in relation to the consequences of not having treatment and the risks of this.

ADVICE, RISKS, OPTIONS AND REFUSAL

The notes should contain detail of the advice given, the risks and the options. If the patient refuses treatment or does not wish to accept the recommended treatment or advice then such refusal should be clearly recorded. The patient may chose not to give a reason why they are refusing treatment (this is, after all, the patient's prerogative). However, the fact that the patient does not wish to give a reason should be recorded.

It must be borne in mind that the health professional should be working in partnership with the patient. They may be able to explore the reasons why treatment is being refused and to reassure the patient, while respecting the patient's right of consent.

LEAFLETS

A patient may have been given leaflets. The content of the leaflet may have been explained to the patient. The patient may have been given leaflets to take away with them. This should be recorded in the notes so that it is clear what advice has been given. The health professional should record details of the leaflets given to the patient including the name of those leaflets.

RECORDING CONSENT AND CHILDREN

It is important to record fully and accurately all matters relating to the consent process regarding children.

In order to record consent issues surrounding children health professionals must a have a good grasp of those issues. The same general principles apply when recording consent issues regarding children. Be particularly clear when recording issues regarding who consented and parental responsibility, whether the child or parents consent has been overruled by the other. Whether there is any disagreement between the child and parents. The record should include full details relating to best interests, Gillick competence, how it was assessed and decisions made, where consent is refused and where there is a dispute.

Consent relating to children is discussed in detail in Chapter 11.

CONSENT FORMS

Health professionals should exercise caution when using standard forms for consent. They can be a useful tool and act as a reminder of the advice that should be given. However, not all of the detail will be on a standard form such as additional risks where the patient had a pre-existing condition. There is a danger that relevant information may be missed either when advising the patient or even if the advice has been given, when it is recorded.

The consent forms may consist of tick boxes. A tick box may read, 'has the patient been advised of the risks?' This tick box lacks the detail required.

It is now more common in standard forms to see the words, 'I confirm the patient has been advised of the following risks . . .' The detailed advice given in respect of the risks can then be clearly recorded.

It is not a defence to say, 'the reason why I did not record detail was that there was no room on the form'. If there is no room on the form, health professionals should write the detail of their advice in the records.

Documenting consent forms are discussed in more detail in Chapter 8, p. 52, under the heading 'In writing'.

The Department of Health has published 'Reference Guide to Consent for Examination or Treatment'[1] and 'Information to Assist in Amending Consent Forms'.[2] These publications contain standard consent forms which can be used or adapted by the Trusts or health professionals. There are four forms:

1 patient agreement to investigation and treatment
2 patient agreement to investigation and treatment of a child or young person
3 patient/parental agreement to investigation and treatment (procedures where consciousness is not impaired)
4 adults who are unable to consent to investigation and treatment.

A careful record should be made of who signed the consent form if, for example, the patient is a child.

DOCUMENTING VERBAL CONSENT

Where consent has been obtained verbally this should be recorded in the notes. For example, a care plan has been agreed to by the patient. An entry in the record should confirm that the care plan was discussed and agreed to and verbal consent was obtained. The care plan must be included in the notes so it is clear what was agreed.

DOCUMENTING CONSENT TO RESEARCH AND REMOVAL OF TISSUE

It is important to document accurately the issues relating to consent and research.

Consent may be recorded in writing on a consent form and signed. Remember a signed consent form itself does not constitute valid consent. All of the other elements must be present, such as voluntariness, sufficient information, capacity and so on.

A good record of the consent process must be recorded regardless of whether there is a signed consent form. Remember to record information such as future storage or use of samples. This should be clearly documented in the patient's records, the laboratory records or both. The record should detail when consent was obtained and the purposes for which the consent was given. (*See also* Chapter 10 on documenting consent issues.)

DOCUMENTING CAPACITY ISSUES

In addition to the general principles of documenting when capacity is in issue health professionals should ensure the detail is recorded very carefully. Include in this detail the findings of the issue of capacity, how the patient's capacity was assessed and whether incapacity is permanent or likely to be long-standing, what is in the patient's best interests and why. These records will be useful for other people involved in the person's care, or if their practice is challenged. Daily notes on an individual's care should be part of this process. Local agency protocols and procedures should cover this.

Where the patient lacks capacity the standard consent form should not be signed by either relatives or healthcare professionals. It is good practice to note, either in the records or in a 'patient unable to consent' form, why the treatment was believed to be in the patient's best interests.

Where a person is judged to lack capacity to consent to day-to-day care, reasonable record keeping regarding capacity is required. If a practitioner's decision is challenged, they must be able to describe why they had a reasonable belief of lack of capacity. The decision about the lack of capacity should always be recorded. Although this does not need to be done on a daily basis, the record should note the decision and should be reviewed regularly. Recording decisions in this way will help staff to demonstrate why they had a reasonable belief in the person's lack of capacity.[3]

EXAMPLE

The care record for Raymond, who is severely disabled by a stroke, might state:

Raymond was unable to tell me whether he wanted a shave today, so a decision was made that a shave would be in his best interests. I will assess his capacity to decide about this again next week, or earlier if he shows signs of improvement.

In order to ensure consent has been validly obtained, consideration should be given to the needs of individuals and families where, for example, English is not their first language, where there are hearing difficulties or they are illiterate. Any difficulties in communicating with the person interviewed and an explanation of how these difficulties were overcome should be recorded.

Capacity is dealt with in detail in Chapter 17.

REFERENCES

1 Department of Health. *Reference Guide to Consent for Examination or Treatment*. 2nd edn. London: Department of Health; 2009. www.dh.gov.uk/prod_consum_dh/groups/ dh_digitalassets/documents/digitalasset/dh_103653.pdf (accessed 20 January 2010).

2 Department of Health. *Information to Assist in Amending Consent Forms*. London: Department of Health; 2005. Available at: www.dh.gov.uk/prod_consum_dh/groups/dh_digitalassets/ documents/digitalasset/dh_103652.pdf (accessed 20 January 2010).

3 Mental Capacity Act, s5; Code of Practice

CHAPTER 11

Consent: children and young persons

Before reading about how consent affects children, consider the following scenario:

> Jacqueline is 15 years old. She is suffering from sickle cell anaemia and her treatment requires her to have a blood transfusion. She is refusing to give consent, but her parents are prepared to give consent in her best interests.

1 Would you treat Jacqueline, or respect her wishes not to treat her?
2 Would it differ if Jacqueline consented to treatment but her parents refused to consent?
3 Would your view differ if Jacqueline were 16 years old?

We will review this at the end of the chapter.

THE LEGAL PERSPECTIVE

A person aged 18 and over, i.e. an adult who is mentally competent, can consent to or refuse treatment. The legal position concerning consent and refusal of treatment by those under the age of 18 is different from the position for adults.

A person with parental responsibility may make treatment choices on behalf of a child. However, where the child has reached 16 years or is Gillick competent, he or she can also give consent to treatment and it is not necessary to consult the parent or guardian. Gillick competency is explained in detail below.

Where a refusal to consent is contrary to the child's best interest, a court may authorise treatment.

As with consent and adults, all the elements must be present so that consent to treat a child is valid, for example, there must be capacity; it must be voluntarily given; sufficient information must have been given; the information must be understood, etc. What differs with children is that it is possible that someone else may consent on the child's behalf. Once a child reaches the age of 18, they are an adult and no one else can consent on their behalf.

In practice

Sometimes health professionals are faced with practical difficulties. When babies and children are being cared for by health professionals it may not always seem practical to seek their parents' consent on every occasion for every routine intervention such as blood tests, urine tests or X-rays. However, it is a legal requirement to obtain valid consent, and health professionals should discuss in advance what routine procedures will be necessary to obtain it.

If valid consent is not obtained the health professional will be accountable.

How does consent for children operate?

Throughout history a child was regarded as the property of its parents and viewed simply as part of their goods and chattels to do with as they wished. Parental rights were paramount. Parents knew what was best for their own children, and they could delegate the responsibility to others if they chose. Physical punishment was essential to establish obedience – everybody knew that. The family was a sacred enclave into which no legislator dared to tread. Even as the impetus that led to the establishment of the Society for the Prevention of Cruelty to Children was taking off, a reformer, Whatley Cooke-Taylor, proclaimed in 1874, 'I would far rather see even a higher rate of infant mortality prevailing . . . than intrude one iota on the sanctity of the domestic hearth'.[1] Prior to the Children Act (1989)[2] legal terminology continued to embody the notion of parents' rights over children.

Today, the role of the parent or guardian is to act as trustee to the child. Their duty is to safeguard the child's rights and interests until the child can take responsibility and exercise judgment for him or herself. The report of an inquiry into the case of Jasmine Beckford was entitled 'A Child in Trust'[3] The title encapsulates the present legal position.

It therefore follows that the appropriate person to take responsibility for and to safeguard the child, is the parent or guardian (i.e. those with parental responsibility). If that person fails to discharge his responsibilities appropriately, and as a result the child is at risk, the law will come into play to protect the child and to secure the transfer of parental responsibility.

A child cannot sue or be sued. Any action will be brought on behalf of a child by the parent or guardian who acts for them until the child is 18, known as a 'litigation friend'. However, there are circumstances where a child may conduct proceedings without a litigation friend such as in family proceedings where, for example, a solicitor considers that the child is able, having regard to his understanding, to give instructions in relation to the proceedings.[4]

Seeking consent

As with adults, seeking consent should be seen as an ongoing process, rather than a one-off event. For any procedure seeking consent does not simply consist of asking for a signature shortly before surgery. Consent is an ongoing process. The whole process of discussing options and coming to a decision should be seen as part of the consent process. Information about the risks of treatment should be discussed early on in this process, and not presented at the last minute when it is too late for it to be considered properly.

Child patients and their parents who have given consent to a particular intervention are entitled to change their minds and withdraw their consent at any point. However, if you have started a procedure, such as an operation under local anaesthetic, and it would be dangerous to stop at that point, it would be lawful to continue until any risk to the child is over. Withdrawal of consent in such circumstances may reflect fear or pain, rather than genuine refusal, and you should do all you can to reassure the patient. This is discussed further below and in detail in Chapters 6 and 15.

Sometimes, during an operation, it may become clear that the child would benefit from an additional procedure, for which consent has not been obtained. You must obtain further consent for this procedure before going ahead, unless the delay involved in doing so would genuinely put the child's life or health at risk. This is discussed in detail in Chapter 9, 'Additional procedures'.

BEST INTERESTS

Any treatment proposed must be in the child's best interest. This is usually determined by the treating health professionals.

There may be occasions where no one is able to give valid consent to treatment, for example, where a child is unconscious after an accident and needs treatment urgently, but no one with parental responsibility can be contacted, or because the child is homeless or is an unaccompanied refugee, and does not have capacity to give consent for him or herself, or the person with parental responsibility may not be competent to give or withhold consent because they are under the influence of alcohol, drugs, or extremely distressed because the child is seriously ill, or the mother of a child is herself under 16 and is not competent to make that particular decision.

In such circumstances, if there is no one else with parental responsibility available and the treatment cannot wait, it is lawful to provide immediately necessary treatment on the basis that it is in the child's best interests.

However, all attempts must be made to ensure that as soon as the child or parents are able to make a decision, their consent to further treatment is sought.

A child or person with parental responsibility cannot compel a health professional to uphold their wishes if the health professional believes they are contrary to the child's best interests.

The court cannot order a doctor to treat a child, the court can only authorise the doctors to treat the minor in accordance with their clinical judgments.[5]

There is no obligation to treat where treatment is futile and thus considered by the treating clinicians not to be in the best interests of the child. These views can, however, be reviewed by the court.

Where it has been determined that treatment is in the child's best interest then consent comes into play.

INVOLVING CHILDREN AND YOUNG PEOPLE IN THE CONSENT PROCESS

Health professionals should involve children and young people as much as possible in discussions about their care, even if they are not able to make decisions on their own.

A child or young person's ability to make decisions depends more on their ability to understand and weigh up options, than on their age. This is discussed in detail below.

Where children are not able to give valid consent for themselves, it is nevertheless very important to involve them as much as possible in decisions about their own health. Even very young children will have opinions about their healthcare, and health professionals should use methods appropriate to their age and understanding to enable these views to be taken into account. A child who is unable to understand any aspects of the healthcare decision may still be able to express preferences about who goes with them to the clinic or what toys or comforters they would like to have with them while they are there. As previously mentioned where treatment choices involve multiple decisions, children may be able to consent to some aspects of their care, even where they are not able to make a decision on the treatment as a whole.

Parents may be unsure about how much information they want their child to have, particularly when a young child is seriously ill, the health professional will need to discuss this in a sensitive manner.

Decision-making with older children will often be a matter of negotiation between the child, those with parental responsibility and clinicians. Children should never feel that decisions are being made over their heads.

CAN A CHILD CONSENT FOR THEMSELVES?

In certain circumstances children can consent for themselves. It is, however, possible to impose treatment on a child without their consent.

Under 18 years

As the child develops and has an increased understanding, his or her wishes will be taken into account. However, the child does not become autonomous until they have reached the age of 18 years.

The Children Act 1989

The Children Act 1989 sets out the duties and responsibilities owed to children by parents and other bodies. It does not, however, set out the child's rights. It is only by a process of deduction that if there is a duty there must be a corresponding right of the child. Although it can be argued that the child must have rights, the reality is that power and authority rests with the parent or guardian who is required to act in the best interests of the child. The Children Act 1989 states that when any question with respect to the upbringing of a child . . . 'the child's welfare shall be the court's paramount consideration'.[6]

Until a child is 18, any consent for surgery, medical or dental treatment will come from the parent or guardian.

Young persons aged 16 and 17

The strict legal position that consent for a person under 18 must come from a parent or guardian has been modified by the Family Law Reform Act 1969.[7]

Family Law Reform Act 1969

Section 8 of the Family Law Reform Act 1969 states:

> (1) The consent of a minor who has attained the age of sixteen years to any surgical, medical or dental treatment which, in the absence of consent, would constitute a trespass to his person, shall be as effective as it would be if he were of full age; and where a minor has by virtue of this section given an effective consent to any treatment it shall not be necessary to obtain any consent for it from his parent or guardian.
>
> (2) In this section 'surgical, medical or dental treatment' includes any procedure undertaken for the purposes of diagnosis, and this section applies to any procedure (including, in particular, the administration of an anaesthetic) which is ancillary to any treatment as it applies to that treatment.
>
> (3) Nothing in this section shall be construed as making ineffective any consent which would have been effective if this section had not been enacted.

This has the effect that young persons aged 16 or 17 are entitled to consent to their own medical treatment. Medical treatment is defined widely and includes all treatment, nursing care and any ancillary procedures involved in that treatment, such as an anaesthetic. It should be noted that it applies to therapeutic treatment. Non-therapeutic procedures are discussed later in this chapter.

Consent will be valid only if it is given voluntarily by an appropriately informed patient capable of consenting to the particular intervention. However, unlike adults, the refusal of a competent person aged 16–17 may in certain circumstances be overridden by either a person with parental responsibility or a court.[8]

Section 8 of the Family Law Reform Act applies only to the young person's own treatment. It does not apply to an intervention, which is not potentially of direct health benefit to the young person, such as blood donation or non-therapeutic research on the causes of a disorder. However, a young person may be able to consent to such an intervention under the standard of Gillick competence, or Mental Capacity Act 2005[9] which is considered further below.

From the age of 16 a young person can be presumed to have capacity to make most decisions about their treatment and care. In order to establish whether a young person aged 16 or 17 has the requisite capacity to consent to the proposed intervention; the same criteria as for adults should be used.

If the requirements for valid consent are met, i.e. that it is voluntary, they have received the required information, etc., it is not legally necessary to obtain consent from a person with parental responsibility for the young person in addition to that of the young person. It is, however, good practice to involve the young person's family in the decision-making process, unless the young person specifically wishes to exclude them.

The Family Law Reform Act 1969, section 8 has the effect that a child who has attained his or her 16th birthday can give effective consent to surgery, medical or dental treatment. However, it goes on to say, 'nothing in this section shall be construed as making ineffective any consent which would have been effective if this section had not been enacted'. Therefore, notwithstanding the child can consent to treatment, it does not invalidate consent given by a parent. What that means is that from birth to 16 years, consent will come from the parent or guardian. From 18 years onwards, consent will come from the young person, as they are now an adult, but from 16 to 18 two consents are possible, either the parent/guardian, or the young person.

The law remains silent about what happens in the event of a conflict. In reality this is not a problem provided that consent is an authority to proceed with treatment, as it does not confer a power of veto. It does not matter which party has given consent, either the parent/guardian, or the young person, it will be lawful to proceed with treatment. Thus the parent may overrule the young persons wishes.

In practice, some conflicts can be difficult for health professionals. What should a health professional do when confronted with a burly 17-year-old who adamantly refuses treatment and his mother cowering behind saying 'yes, go ahead'. The health professional may well decide that it is better to be prudent than merely courageous!

EXAMPLE

What would the legal position be if John, a 16-year-old, refuses a life-saving blood transfusion because he is a Jehovah's Witness and the parents, not sharing his religious view, will consent to his treatment? What should the health professional do?

The health professional will be concerned that if they respect John's wishes and not intervene that he will die and also whether in these circumstances the parents would sue. The parents may well decide to sue the health professional, whether a claim would succeed will very much depend on the circumstances. Did John have capacity to give valid consent, was he given the requisite information to make a decision, did he understand it? Remember, if the parents have consented to treatment then the health professional can proceed with the treatment lawfully. The health professional may consider, where there is a dispute of such a serious nature, the matter be brought before the attention of the court to determine. The court can overrule the wishes of the child. Referrals to the court are discussed later in Chapter 21.

Young persons and the Mental Health Act

Where detention of a young person to a psychiatric hospital is concerned, the Mental Health Act 2007, section 43,[10] has impacted on the issue of consent. The Act states:

> **Informal admission of patients aged 16 or 17**
>
> In section 131 of the 1983 Act (informal admission of patients), for subsection (2) substitute –
>
> '(2) Subsections (3) and (4) below apply in the case of a patient aged 16 or 17 years who has capacity to consent to the making of such arrangements as are mentioned in subsection (1) above.
>
> (3) If the patient consents to the making of the arrangements, they may be made, carried out and determined on the basis of that consent even though there are one or more persons who have parental responsibility for him.
>
> (4) If the patient does not consent to the making of the arrangements, they may not be made, carried out or determined on the basis of the consent of a person who has parental responsibility for him.

(5) In this section –
  (a) the reference to a patient who has capacity is to be read in accordance with the Mental Capacity Act 2005; and
  (b) "parental responsibility" has the same meaning as in the Children Act 1989.'

This has the effect that, as of October 2008, parents are no longer able to give consent to the admission and detention of a young person into a psychiatric hospital. This may lead to a review on the law on overruling the refusal of consent by a young person and cases, such as Re W[11] discussed later, may be challenged so as not to be followed.

TREATING A CHILD IN AN EMERGENCY

EXAMPLE

David, a boy of five years, is brought into the hospital emergency department unconscious, following a road traffic accident. He requires emergency surgery to save his life.

He is accompanied by his seven-year-old brother. Their parents cannot be contacted.

Can David be treated without consent?

Where an emergency situation arises and it is not possible to obtain the consent of the child or person with parental responsibility or the court, health professionals may be justified in treating that child, acting in their best interest in an emergency where treatment is essential to survival or health of the child.

The courts have stated that where consent is not possible from those with parental responsibility, the child or the courts, or where consent is refused by those with parental responsibility despite emergency treatment being in the best interests of the child, doubt should be resolved in favour of preserving life and it will be acceptable to undertake treatment to preserve life or prevent serious damage to health.

The health professional who treats a child in such an emergency would have a defence to an allegation of trespass to the person.

The health professional would be acting without consent but would be justified in an emergency in the best interests of the child in order to save the child's life. The health professional providing the treatment would be protected against any allegation of trespass to the person by the defence that they were acting in an emergency in the child's best interests.[12]

CHILDREN UNDER 16 YEARS

Who can give consent for a child under 16 years? Can a child under the age of 16 years consent for themselves?

From what has been set out above we know that a person with parental responsibility may consent on behalf of a child. The courts have also determined that there are circumstances where a child under the age of 16 years may consent for themselves. A person under 16 may have capacity to make decisions, depending on their maturity and ability to understand what is involved. Parents and the court may overrule the wishes of the child.

A parent may lose the right to consent for their child as the court has held that 'parental rights' did not exist, other than to safeguard the best interests of a child and that in some circumstances a child could consent to treatment, and that in these circumstances a parent had no power to veto treatment.[13]

When determining matters in relation to a child the court will have regard to 'the ascertainable wishes and feelings of the child concerned (considered in the light of his age and understanding)'.[14]

GILLICK COMPETENCE AND FRASER GUIDELINES

The terms 'Gillick competence' and 'Fraser guidelines' comes from the case of Gillick v West Norfolk and Wisbech AHA and the DHSS 1985.[15]

Gillick competence

The Gillick case was brought in relation to the production of a circular issued by the Department of Health and Social Security in 1974. The circular stated that contraceptive services should be more readily available to girls who were under 16 because of emerging statistics showing a rise in the number of births and induced abortions among girls of such age. The circular stated that in certain circumstances a doctor could lawfully prescribe contraception to a girl under 16 years without the consent of her parents. Mrs Gillick objected to the content of the circular and wrote a letter to the administrator which stated:

> I formally forbid any medical staff employed by Norfolk Area Health Authority to give any contraceptive or abortion advice or treatment whatsoever to my four daughters whilst they are under 16 years without my consent.

The acting administrator replied, stating that the Area Health Authority held the view that treatment prescribed by a doctor is a matter for that doctor's clinical judgment, taking into account all the factors of the case.

Mrs Gillick brought an action seeking a declaration that the advice in the circular was unlawful and wrong and that it did or may adversely affect the welfare of her children, her right as a parent and her ability to properly discharge her duties as a parent. She also sought a declaration that no doctor or health professional should give contraception, advice or treatment without the consent of the parent.

The House of Lords held that a child under 16 can, in certain circumstances, give a valid consent to medical treatment including contraception or abortion without parental agreement or knowledge. Lord Scarman commented:

> the parental right yields to the child's right to make his own decisions when he reaches a sufficient understanding and intelligence to be capable of making up his own mind on the matter requiring decision.

Thus a child below 16 may lawfully be given general medical advice and treatment without parental agreement, provided that certain criteria are met.

The health professional must:
1 seek to persuade the child to involve the parent or guardian in the decision
2 be satisfied that the child has sufficient maturity to understand the nature, purpose and likely outcome of the proposed treatment
3 the proposed treatment is in the best interests of the young person.

A child is Gillick competent if these criteria are satisfied.

Fraser guidelines

Lord Fraser also presided in the House of Lords case of Gillick. He ruled that it was lawful for doctors to prescribe contraception to under-16s without parental knowledge, as long as certain criteria are followed.

These criteria, known as the Fraser guidelines, require the health professional to be satisfied that:

➤ the young person will understand the professional's advice
➤ the young person cannot be persuaded to inform their parents
➤ the young person is likely to begin, or to continue having, sexual intercourse with or without contraceptive treatment
➤ unless the young person receives contraceptive treatment, their physical or mental health, or both, are likely to suffer
➤ the young person's best interests require them to receive contraceptive advice or treatment with or without parental consent.

The difference between 'Gillick competence' and 'Fraser guidelines'

The term 'Gillick competence' applies to under-16s and their capacity to consent to their own treatment and is considered to apply to all treatment, including abortion.

Fraser guidelines are concerned with contraception and the criteria the health professional must satisfy him/herself that the under-16 meets to prescribe contraception.

The rulings were specifically for doctors, but are also considered to apply to other health professionals, including nurses. They may also be interpreted to cover youth workers and health promotion workers.

For the purpose of further discussion, the term 'Gillick competence' is used.

Applying the criteria for Gillick competency

One of the difficulties is to determine how much effort must be made to involve the parents in the consent process. If the child is Gillick competent and is able to give voluntary consent after receiving appropriate information, that consent will be valid and additional consent by a person with parental responsibility will not be required. Where the decision will have ongoing implications, such as long-term use of contraception, it is good practice to encourage the child to inform her parents unless it would clearly not be in the child's best interests to do so.

Another difficulty is to determine to what extent the child can consent, for example, a tooth extraction or brain surgery. The Gillick case determined that provided that child has achieved sufficient maturity to understand fully what is proposed, a doctor acting on such grounds will be immune from civil action for trespass to the person or criminal prosecution. As the understanding required for different interventions will vary considerably, a child under 16 may therefore have the capacity to consent to some interventions but not others. The greater the medical complexity a greater understanding by the child will be required. As with adults, an assumption that a child with a learning disability may not be able to understand the issues should never be made. However, in some cases, for example, because of a mental disorder, a child's mental state may fluctuate significantly so that on some occasions the child appears Gillick competent in respect of a particular decision and on other occasions does not. Careful consideration should be given to whether the child is truly Gillick competent at the time to take this decision.

In the case of Re R (A Minor),[16] a 15-year-old girl who lacked insight into her acute psychiatric condition was held not to be Gillick competent. The illness itself prevented her from fully understanding the need for medication in order to control her condition and was deemed to lack the necessary maturity and competence to make the decision herself.

In summary, consent for a child under 16 years may come from someone with parental responsibility or they may consent for themselves if they are deemed Gillick competent. They are competent if they have sufficient understanding and intelligence to enable them to understand fully what is involved in a proposed intervention. As the understanding required for different interventions will vary considerably, a child under 16 may therefore have the capacity to consent to some interventions but not others. A child's capacity may fluctuate and careful consideration should be given to whether the child is truly Gillick competent at the time the decision is made.

If the child consents it is valid and it is not necessary to obtain the additional consent of the parents. Remember, though, it is good practice to encourage the child to involve the parents.

EXAMPLE

Maria is 15 and pregnant by her 16-year-old boyfriend. She wants an abortion, but does not want her parents to know about it. The health professionals involved in her care have tried without success to persuade her to involve her family. After several discussions with Maria, the treating doctor is satisfied that she fully understands the implications of having or not having an abortion and is very clear in her own mind what she wants. She is therefore competent to consent for herself. Maria is adamant that she does not want to involve her parents. The doctor is also convinced that, in the short term at least, it is impossible to persuade her to talk to her parents, but he strongly encourages her to involve another adult whom she trusts for support.

As Maria is Gillick competent and they have followed the guidelines set out in the Gillick judgment and further pursuant to fulfilling the requirements under the Abortion Act 1967, the abortion can go ahead.[17]

The health professionals involved should ensure that Maria is aware of ongoing sources of confidential support and advice, in both sexual health and wider health matters, such as that provided by her school nurse, her GP and local contraceptive clinic.

In summary, to determine Gillick competence:

➤ the treatment must be in the best interests of the child
➤ the health professional must seek to persuade the child to involve the parent or guardian in the decision
➤ the health professional will need to be satisfied that the child has sufficient maturity to understand the nature, purpose and likely outcome of the proposed treatment.

English law does not recognise the 'emancipation of minors' in the same way that they do in America. For example, a 15-year-old who ran away from home and has been self-supporting for the last two years does not become emancipated. Nor does marriage emancipate a 16-year-old. Therefore, regardless of their independence, the same rules relating to minors still applies.

CONSENT MUST BE VOLUNTARY

Where a child or young person has the capacity to give consent, valid consent must be given voluntarily. This requirement must be considered carefully. Children and young people may be subject to undue influence by their parents, other carers, or a potential sexual partner, and it is important to establish that the decision is that of the individual him or herself.

HOW MUCH INFORMATION SHOULD CHILDREN AND PARENTS BE GIVEN?

The child or young person must be given sufficient information in order to weigh up and make a decision. This is discussed in Chapter 9 and applies equally to children as those with parental responsibility.

Children and their parents should be given enough information so they can decide whether to consent to, or refuse, treatment. For example, they may need to know:

➤ the benefits and the risks of the proposed treatment
➤ what the treatment will involve
➤ the implications of not having the treatment
➤ what alternatives may be available
➤ the practical effects on their lives of having, or not having, the treatment.

It is important that the information is provided in a manner that the child or parent can understand, and the health professional is content that they have understood it. This may involve explaining what is proposed in language which is suited to the child's age and abilities, using pictures, toys and play activity where appropriate and drawing on the skills of specialist colleagues. The information should be provided at the child's own pace, allowing time and opportunity to answer questions and to address concerns, fears and expectations, unless it is an emergency. It may also involve using interpreters, where the child's, or their parents', first language is not English. If an interpreter is necessary, asking the child or any family member to interpret for their parents should be avoided.

Where a child has a disability, the health professional should take particular care to ensure that the information is provided in a suitable form, involving, for example, interpreters for hearing impaired children or appropriate materials for those with learning disabilities. Specialist colleagues may be able to act as facilitators or advocates where children have particular needs. Parents are useful in assisting in communicating with their child who has a disability.

Health professionals should never assume that a child with a disability is not able to consent for themselves. Every opportunity must be made to assist the child in making their own decisions.

CAN CONSENT BY A CHILD BE OVERRIDDEN?

Where a child has the power to consent to treatment either where they are 16 or 17 under the provisions of the Family Law Reform Act 1969 or where they are under 16 under the Gillick case their consent to treatment cannot be overridden by a parent.

REFUSAL OF TREATMENT

As previously mentioned a person of 16 or 17 years can consent to treatment in accordance with section 8 of the Family Law Reform Act or a child under 16 who is Gillick competent can consent to treatment, but can they refuse treatment?

Their rights under the Family Law Reform Act or Gillick guidelines confers a right to consent to treatment. It does not confer a right to refuse treatment.

Refusal of treatment by a person under 16 years

Where a person under the age of 16, but Gillick competent, refuses treatment, such a refusal can be overruled either by a person with parental responsibility for the child or by the court. If more than one person has parental responsibility for the young person, consent by any one such person is sufficient, irrespective of the refusal of any other individual.

Child or young person with capacity refusing treatment

As with a person under 16 years, where a young person refuses treatment this can be overruled by a person with parental responsibility for the child or by the court. If more than one person has parental responsibility for the young person, consent by any of them is sufficient, irrespective of the refusal of any other individual.

In the case of Re W,[18] an anorexic below 18 years, the court directed that she should be moved to a specialist hospital to be fed even though she was refusing. The court of appeal held that section 8 of the Family Law Reform Act did not prevent consent being given by the parents or the court. While the child had a right to consent to treatment under the Act, it did not confer a right to refuse treatment that was necessary to save her life.

It is possible, therefore, to impose treatment without the young person's consent.

Under the Children Act 1989 the court must have regard to 'the ascertainable wishes and feelings of the child concerned'. When overruling a child's refusal to consent it must be exercised on the basis that the welfare of the child/young person is paramount. Welfare includes psychological as well as physical health. It is uncertain in what circumstances a child's wishes could be overridden. In the case of Re W her wishes to refuse treatment was overruled by the court as her health was rapidly deteriorating and her life was in danger. The court did not give any clear guidance on what other circumstances would also justify the decision to be overridden. It was, however, stated that a court would be justified in overriding a child's wishes where 'his or her welfare is threatened by a serious and imminent risk that it will suffer grave and irreversible mental or physical harm' or where refusal to treat will in all probability lead to the death of a child or to severe permanent injury. The court also took the wider view that the court could overrule the refusal of treatment whenever the court thinks it is in the child's best interest.

Overruling a child's decision to refuse treatment can have significant implications for the child, for example a child refusing an abortion or chemotherapy with a poor prognosis. Before overruling the child's decision consideration must be given to applying to the court for a ruling prior to undertaking the interventions. Applications to court are discussed in Chapter 21.

In order for a person with parental responsibility to consider overruling a child's decision they will need sufficient information about the child's condition and treatment options, etc. This may be a breach of confidence on the part of the clinician treating the child however, may be justifiable where it is in the child's best interests. Such a justification may only apply where the child is at serious risk as a result of their refusal of treatment. Confidentiality is not explored in detail in this book but health professionals should be familiar with the rules regarding confidentiality.

The recent media attention on a 13-year-old girl, Hannah Jones, successfully battled a hospital decision to forcefully give her a heart transplant for a hole in the heart. She refused the operation and said she understood her decision may lead to her death, but that she didn't want to go through any more operations and understood that there was a chance she would be okay and a chance that she might not be but was willing to take the chance. Doctors had warned her that the transplant itself might lead to her dying on the operating table but insisted she have the operation notwithstanding that there was no strong clinical evidence to support the heart transplant. The hospital eventually abandoned the High Court proceedings after Hannah told them she would not let surgeons operate. She has chosen instead to spend her remaining time at home. It is likely that the hospital reconsidered whether such surgery was in the best interest of the child taking into account her wishes and feelings and physical and psychological effect the operation would have on her.[19] In July 2009, Hannah changed her mind and has since undergone a heart transplant.

Refusing consent where neglect or abuse is suspected

Section 47 of the Children Act 1989[20] confers a duty on the local authority that where a child in the area is:

➤ subject of an emergency protection order/police protection or
➤ they have reasonable cause to suspect a child is suffering or is likely to suffer significant harm.

The authority shall make or cause to be made necessary enquiries to decide whether they should take any action to safeguard or promote the child's welfare.

Where parents do not cooperate and refuse consent to assessment or examination, and abuse or neglect is suspected, if their concerns about the child's safety are not so urgent as to require an emergency protection order, a local authority may apply to court for a child assessment order. In these circumstances, the court may direct the parents/caregivers to cooperate with an assessment of the child, the details of which should be specified. The order does not take away the child's own right to refuse to participate in an assessment, for example a medical examination, so long as he or she is of sufficient age and understanding.

As in other circumstances involving children, the child (if they are Gillick competent) or young persons aged 16–17, can give valid consent. Where the health professional regards the child to be of an age and level of understanding to give her/his own consent, in these circumstances parents must be informed as soon as possible and a full record made at the time. A child who is of sufficient age and understanding may refuse some or all of the medical assessment though refusal can be overridden by the court.

Someone with parental responsibility can give valid consent. Wherever possible the permission of a parent for a child under 16 should be obtained prior to any medical assessment and/or other medical treatment even if the child is judged to be of sufficient understanding. If this is not possible or appropriate, then the reasons should be clearly recorded.

Others who may consent in these circumstances include:

➤ the local authority when the child is subject of a care order (though the parent/carer should be informed)

➤ the local authority when the child is accommodated under section 20 of the Children Act 1989[21] and the parent/carers have abandoned the child or are physically or mentally unable to give such authority. When a parent or carer has given general consent authorising medical treatment for the child, legal advice must be taken as to whether this provides consent for a medical assessment for child protection purposes

➤ the High Court has inherent jurisdiction

➤ a Family Proceedings Court as part of a direction attached to an emergency protection order, an interim care order or a child assessment order.

Where circumstances do not allow permission to be obtained and the child needs emergency treatment, the health professional may decide to proceed without consent.

In non-emergency situations when parental permission is not obtained, the social worker and their line manager should obtain legal advice and consider where it is in the child's best interest to seek a court order.

Child or young person without capacity

Capacity is decision specific, so a child may be competent to decide on some aspects of their care or treatment but not to others. It should not be assumed that if a child does not have capacity to consent to some aspect that they must lack capacity to consent to any aspect of their care. Each time a decision is made capacity must be considered.

Where a child lacks capacity to consent to treatment, consent can be given on their behalf by any one person with parental responsibility or by the court. Those giving consent on behalf of child patients must have the capacity to consent to the intervention in question, they must be acting voluntarily, and be appropriately informed. When consent is given on behalf of the child the treatment or intervention must be in the child's best interests, the child's best interests is paramount.

Notwithstanding a child may lack capacity to consent for themselves it is good practice to involve the child as much as possible in the decision-making process.

THE MENTAL CAPACITY ACT 2005 AND THE EFFECT ON CHILDREN AND YOUNG PEOPLE

Set out below is an overview as to how the Mental Capacity Act[22] applies to children. The Mental Capacity Act 2005 is discussed in detail in Chapter 17 and should be cross referenced for detailed information.

The Mental Capacity Act and young people aged 16–17 years

The Mental Capacity Act 2005 applies to young people aged 16–17 years, who may lack capacity to make specific decisions, however, there are three exceptions:

1 Unlike an adult, a person under 18 cannot make a Lasting Power of Attorney. Only people aged 18 and over can make a Lasting Power of Attorney

2 A person under 18 cannot make an advance decision to refuse medical treatment.

3 The Court of Protection cannot make a statutory will for a person aged under 18.

Health professionals undertaking the care or treatment of a young person aged 16–17 who lacks capacity will generally have protection from liability as long as the person carrying out the act:[23]

➤ has taken reasonable steps to establish that the young person lacks capacity

➤ reasonably believes that the young person lacks capacity and that the act is in the young person's best interests, and

➤ follows the Act's principles.

When assessing the young person's best interests, the person providing care or treatment must consult those involved in the young person's care and anyone interested in their welfare, if it is practical and appropriate to do so.

This may include the young person's parents. Care should be taken not to breach the young person's right to confidentiality.

If there is a disagreement about the care, treatment or welfare of a young person aged 16 or 17 who lacks capacity to make relevant decisions. Depending on the circumstances, the case may be heard in court.

The Mental Capacity Act and children under 16 years

The Mental Capacity Act 2005 does not apply to children aged under 16 who do not have capacity. Generally speaking, people with parental responsibility for such children will be making decisions on their behalf already. The Act is only therefore of limited potential application to brain injured children.

The provisions of the Act will assist the parents of brain injured children to prepare for the future by considering decisions which may need to be made in advance of their child reaching 16 years of age, if she or he is unlikely to have the requisite mental capacity at that point.

This could include the appointment of someone to look after the child's affairs, when they are older, and when the parents may no longer be able or be around to make such decisions.

While the Act does not generally apply to people under the age of 16 there are two exceptions:

1 The Court of Protection can make decisions about a child's property or finances (or appoint a deputy to make these decisions) if the child lacks capacity to make such decisions within section 2(1) of the Act and is likely to still lack capacity to make financial decisions when they reach the age of 18.[24]

2 Offences of ill treatment or wilful neglect of a person who lacks capacity also applies to victims younger than 16.[25]

PARENTAL RESPONSIBILITY

Scope of parental responsibility

Parental responsibility refers to the rights and responsibilities that a person has in respect of their children. The Children Act 1989 sets out the obligations of those with parental responsibility. The child's welfare is paramount and if those with parental responsibility do not discharge this obligation it allows the courts to step in to ensure the child's welfare is being dealt with as a matter of paramount importance. It is this that allows the court to step in and make a decision where the parent is refusing treatment against the best interest of the child. It is considered that the parents are not discharging their obligations under the Act.

In order for a person with parental responsibility to discharge their duty to act in the best interest of the child it follows that they require information about their child's health in order to care for and make decisions about their child's treatment. They have a right to request disclosure of information about their child held by healthcare professionals. Those with parental responsibility also have a statutory right to apply for access to their children's health records, unless the child is capable of consenting for themselves.

These rights exist in order to allow those with parental responsibility to exercise their duty of care towards their child. As the child becomes competent to make more decisions for him/herself, the extent of the parents' rights to act on the child's behalf diminishes. Where the child is capable of consenting for him/herself disclosure of information may be a breach of confidentiality.

Who has parental responsibility?

Parental responsibility is defined as 'all the rights, duties, powers, responsibilities and authority, which by law a parent of a child has in relation to the child and his property'.[26] Parental responsibility includes the right to refuse and consent to treatment.

We have discussed the circumstances where someone with parental responsibility for the child may consent to their treatment. But who has parental responsibility?

It is often presumed by health professionals that those caring for a child automatically have parental responsibility when sometimes they in fact do not. An example may be the biological father who nevertheless may not have parental responsibility. If the health professional were to ask the biological father if they have parental responsibility it would be no surprise if they answered 'yes' genuinely believing it to be the case. This can leave the health professional vulnerable because if the father does not have parental responsibility then the health professional would have treated a child without valid consent and will be accountable.

More than one person can have parental responsibility for a child and parental responsibility does not automatically cease on divorce. Some people may acquire parental responsibility through marriage or the court. Thus it is possible that many people may have parental responsibility over the same child, such as the biological father and step fathers. Parental responsibility is shared between those that have it, but individuals can act alone and without the others in meeting responsibilities to safeguard and protect the child. Parents with parental responsibility are entitled to be consulted in educational and medical matters concerning their children.

The Children Act 1989 and other legislation sets out persons who may have parental responsibility. These include:

➤ Both the child's father and mother, if they are married to each other at the time of conception or birth.[27] It is the child's gestational mother who has parental responsibility; the woman who gives birth to the child. The age of the mother has no impact on her parental responsibility in law. Thus an 11-year-old child who has given birth will have parental responsibility for her baby.

➤ The child's mother, but not father if they were not married at the time of birth unless the father has acquired parental responsibility via a court order or a parental responsibility agreement or the couple subsequently marry.[28]

The law in this area has since been revised. For children whose births were registered from 15 April 2002 in Northern Ireland, from 4 May 2006 in Scotland, and from 1 December 2003 in England and Wales parental responsibility rests with both parents, provided they are named on the birth certificate, regardless of whether they are married or not by jointly registering the birth of the child with the mother.[29]

For children whose births are registered prior to these dates, the father would only automatically have parental responsibility if he was married to the mother. Otherwise, he could acquire parental responsibility through a Parental Responsibility Agreement with the mother[30] or a Parental Responsibility Order through the courts.[31] A married step-parent or civil partner may also obtain parental responsibility in this way.

➤ If the parents are divorced, both parents retain parental responsibility for the child.

➤ Parental responsibility is lost by those giving the child up for adoption. When the child has been formally adopted, the adoptive parents take on parental responsibility.

➤ Where the child was conceived by assisted reproduction: legal parentage in these circumstances is addressed by the Human Fertilisation and Embryology Act 1990.[32] Specific advice should be sought for individual cases.

➤ If the child is the subject of a care order, the local authority has parental responsibility which is shared with the parents. If the child is in care voluntarily, parental responsibility remains with the parents.

➤ The child's legally appointed guardian by the court acquires parental responsibility.

➤ A person in whose favour the court has made a residence or care order concerning the child; a local authority designated in a care order in respect of the child, acquires parental responsibility.

➤ A local authority or other authorised person who holds an emergency protection order in respect of the child acquires parental responsibility.

➤ Foster parents do not automatically have parental responsibility.

➤ Grandparents do not have parental responsibility of a grandchild unless gained through a court order.

Delegating parental responsibility

EXAMPLE

Tommy is four years old. He falls off the slide at nursery school. He has a small cut above his eye, which is bleeding. They have made telephone calls to Tommy's parents but they cannot get hold of them. The nursery teacher takes him to the local walk-in centre.

Can health professionals at the walk-in centre treat Tommy without the consent of the parents?

Those with parental responsibility may delegate particular responsibilities to others. The Children Act 1989 allows a person who has parental responsibility for a child to arrange for some or all of their parental responsibility to be met by one or more persons acting on his behalf,[33] for example authorising a school to give treatment for minor ailments. In an emergency, a person without parental responsibility – for example, a grandparent or childminder – may do 'what is reasonable in all the circumstances of the case for the purpose of safeguarding or promoting the child's welfare'. This could include giving consent to urgent medical treatment.

EXAMPLE

A group of children aged 12–14 is taken on a school camping trip.

The school seeks explicit agreement in advance from the children's parents that the teachers in charge may consent to any treatment which becomes immediately necessary during the trip. Part way through the holiday, Mark, who is 12 years old, suffers an asthma attack during the night and is unable to communicate. A teacher takes him to the local hospital. Mark needs treatment with a nebuliser. The teacher is able to consent on his behalf to treatment as he has authority from Mark's parents to exercise parental responsibility. This avoids the necessity of trying to track down Mark's parents urgently by phone before the treatment is given.

However, all reasonable action should be taken to contact his parents so that they can be appropriately involved in any follow-up care.

WHERE THERE IS A DISAGREEMENT

Consent to treatment is valid if it comes from the child, as set out above, or from a person with parental responsibility. This means that if the minor is competent to consent then that is sufficient; if not, then consent from someone with parental responsibility is sufficient. Therefore, consent given by one person is valid, even if the child or another person with parental responsibility withholds consent. If there is a dispute between, for example, the mother and the father, provided one person with authority gives consent, the health professional can lawfully proceed with treatment.

Where children and those with parental responsibility do not agree

There may be times when children and those with parental responsibility for them do not agree on whether the child should have a particular procedures or treatment.

The decision of a competent child to accept treatment cannot be over-ridden by a person with parental responsibility. However, if the child refuses treatment, those with parental responsibility may consent on their behalf, and treatment can lawfully be given. This power to overrule a competent child's refusal should be used lightly, bearing in mind both the consequences of forcing treatment on a child who has refused it and the consequences of non-treatment in this particular case. Health professionals must always be guided by the best interests of the child.

Where a child is refusing treatment which his or her parents want to accept, and the consequences of refusal are potentially very serious (for example, the foreseeable death of the child), health professionals should consider seeking a court ruling on what would be in the best interests of the child. Courts have the power to overrule the decisions of both children and those with parental responsibility.

Where the consequences are less serious, health professional should assist the child and their parents reach agreement.

Similarly, there may be differences of opinion between parents and non-competent children. While, legally, the consent of the person with parental responsibility is sufficient for health professional to proceed, it is clearly good practice to do everything possible to reach agreement. In many cases, it may be possible to delay treatment until the child is content for it to go ahead. Again, health professionals should always be guided by the child's best interests.

Where parents do not agree with each other

As previously stated the consent of any one person with parental responsibility is sufficient for treatment lawfully to be given, even if another person with parental responsibility does not agree. For example, one parent may not agree to the MMR being given while the other parent may agree. Clearly, consensus between those with parental responsibility should be achieved if at all possible.

While consent of only one party is required in law, it is good practice to consider the views of both parents if there is a disagreement. Where there is disagreement, the parties should try to reach a consensus. If the matter cannot be resolved by discussion and mutual agreement, it may be necessary to seek a view from the courts.

If agreement cannot be reached, the health professional must exercise his professional judgment as to what is in the best interests of the child. If the matter under consideration is complex, or there are potentially serious implications for the child, a second opinion should be sought and consideration given to seeking the authority of the court. If there is dispute over controversial procedures, for example male circumcision, the health professional should not proceed without the authority of the court.

It has been held by the court that there is a 'small group of important decisions' that should only be carried out where both parents agree. If they do not agree, the court should decide whether the procedure or treatment is in the best interest of the child.[34]

The case of Re J concerned the circumcision of a male infant, which the Muslim father wanted performed against the wishes of the non-Muslim mother. The court held that circumcision was being sought for social and cultural reasons, rather than medical necessity, but accepted that nonetheless this was normally a matter for the parents to decide. In this case the court concluded that circumcision should not be performed.

Where those with parental responsibility disagree as to whether non-therapeutic procedures are in the child's best interests, it is advisable to refer the decision to the courts.

It is recommended that certain important decisions, such as sterilisation for contraceptive purposes, should be referred to the courts for guidance, even if those with parental responsibility consent to the operation going ahead.

Those with parental responsibility consenting on behalf of a child must themselves have capacity in order for consent to be valid.

Where health professionals and those with parental responsibility do not agree

Circumstances may arise where health professionals and parents do not agree on what is best for a child.

If parents refuse treatment for their child and the child cannot consent for themselves, usually the treatment will not go ahead. However, if it believed by the health professionals that it is crucial for the child to have the treatment in question, for example if the child would die or suffer serious permanent injury without it, an application can be made to the courts to decide what is in the child's best interests. Applications to court can be made at short notice if necessary. If the emergency is such that there is no time to apply to court, any doubts should be resolved in favour of the preservation of life. Dealing with an emergency situation is discussed later in this chapter.

Conversely, the situation may arise where health professionals believe that the treatment the parents want is not appropriate, for example where a child is very seriously ill, and health professionals believe that the suffering involved in further treatment would outweigh the possible benefits. Parents cannot compel health professionals to provide particular treatment if it is not considered to be clinically appropriate. In these circumstances it would be prudent to ask the courts to rule if agreement cannot be reached. While a court would not require the health professional to provide treatment against their clinical judgment, it could require them to transfer responsibility for the child's care to another clinician who does believe that the proposed treatment is appropriate.[35]

Parental responsibility and ward of court

Where a child is a ward of court, no important step can be taken for the child without the prior consent of the court. This is likely to include significant medical interventions. Consent would not be required for minor injuries or common childhood diseases.

A child who is themselves a mother: a young mother

A mother usually has parental responsibility for its own child and thus can decide whether to consent or refuse treatment of her child. What is the position where the mother is her herself a child? The young mother herself may not, due to her age, be able to consent to her own treatment; consent to her treatment must therefore come from her parents. In these circumstances can the child who is a young mother, give consent for her own child? Or should consent be sought from her own parents, i.e. the grandparents of the baby?

The child's gestational mother has parental responsibility and the age of the mother has no impact on her parental responsibility in law. A grandparent only has parental responsibility for their child, i.e. the young mother. Grandparents do not automatically have parental responsibility of the grandchild unless a court order has been obtained.

Health professionals often take the precaution of obtaining consent from both the young mother and the grandparents who have parental responsibility. The judges in the Gillick case determined that provided the young mother had the requisite mental capacity to consent to treatment on the baby's behalf then it would be valid.

Whether or not the young mother has capacity will depend on the seriousness of the decisions to be made. The young mother therefore may have capacity to consent to some things but not for others. Any procedure or treatment must of course be in the best interests of the baby.

If the young mother does not have capacity to consent for her baby's treatment then consent must come from someone who does have it, such as a grandparent who has a court order.

Health professionals must bear in mind that the young mother may be under the care of social services. In these circumstances it may be appropriate to also consult with social services. Social services may or may not have the right to consent for the baby. It is good practice to always involve the young mother in any healthcare decisions regarding the baby.

Parental responsibility in an emergency

In an emergency, it is justifiable to treat a child who lacks capacity without the consent of a person with parental responsibility, if it is not possible to obtain consent in time and if the treatment is necessary to save the child's life or prevent serious deterioration.

If further routine procedures are required, consent should then be sought in the usual way.

INTERVENTIONS THAT DO NOT PHYSICALLY BENEFIT THE CHILD

Where a procedure is suggested that will not physically benefit the particular child, for example, using a child as a bone marrow donor for a sibling, is an example of a procedure that will not physically benefit that particular child. Donation of bone marrow can be painful and carries some significant risks. It is not a minimal intervention. If the child is competent they should make up their own mind as to whether or not they wish to donate.

The test for competence in such cases is the same as for under-16s, i.e. whether they are Gillick competent, whether the child has 'sufficient understanding and intelligence to enable him or her to understand fully what is proposed'.

Where children are not competent to decide for themselves, someone with parental responsibility can consent on their behalf, but only if the intervention is in the best interests of the child who will be undergoing the non-therapeutic intervention. While children lacking capacity have on some occasions provided bone marrow to assist in the treatment of a sibling, it is not lawful to balance the interests of the child in need of the transplant with the interests of the potential child donor. It will clearly be very difficult for the parents of a seriously ill child to take a dispassionate view of the best interests of the child's healthy sibling. It is therefore good practice to provide independent scrutiny of the parents' decision, for example, through an independent assessor or consideration of the case in a hospital clinical ethics committee. The legal test is whether donating bone marrow is in the best interests of the healthy child. Without such dispassionate assessment the treatment may not be lawful. If there is any doubt as to the best interests of the healthy child, a court ruling should be sought.

REMOVAL OF TISSUE FROM A CHILD

The Human Tissue Act 2004[36] sets out the legal framework for the storage and use of tissue from the living and for the removal, storage and use of tissue and organs from the dead. This includes 'residual' tissue following clinical and diagnostic procedures.

The Act does not deal directly with the removal of tissue from the living. The process of seeking consent for the storage and use of tissue from patients, including children, will be dealt with under the usual rules of consent.

The Act sets out a schedule of purposes for which tissue maybe taken.[37] They include, for example, anatomical examination, obtaining scientific or medical information which may be relevant to any other person, research in connection with disorders, or the functioning of the human body and transplantation.

Anyone removing, storing or using material in circumstances for which the Act requires consent, must be satisfied that the consent is in place.

A child's or person's agreement or refusal to consent to the donation, storage or use of tissue for purposes under the Act must not affect the investigation or treatment that they receive.

Under the Act, a child is defined as being under 18 years old. Children may consent to a proposed medical procedure or the storage and use of their tissue if they are Gillick competent.

A person who has parental responsibility for the child can consent on his or her behalf only if the child has not made a decision and:

➤ is not competent to do so; or
➤ chooses not to make that decision, although he or she is competent to do so.

A person who has parental responsibility is discussed in detail ante.

It is good practice to consult the person who has parental responsibility for the child and to involve them in the process of the child making a decision. As with other decisions made by children, it is important to make sure that the child has consented voluntarily and has not been unduly influenced by anyone else.

If there is any dispute between persons with parental responsibility or any doubt as to the child's best interests, the matter should be referred to court for approval.

CHILDREN AND CONSENT TO RESEARCH

The law differentiates between therapeutic research, for example an untested treatment, which might be better than existing treatment, and non-therapeutic research, for example the taking of additional blood samples with no therapeutic benefit to the child.

For therapeutic research, a competent child or a person with parental responsibility, can give consent. For non-therapeutic research, the procedure cannot go ahead if the child withholds consent, irrespective of their age and of the views of those with parental responsibility.

Therapeutic research

Parents may often be invited to consent to their child being involved in 'therapeutic research', on the basis that a new treatment may be as effective, or more effective, than the standard treatment. Parents must be given sufficient information to ensure that they understand what is involved in the proposed research. In particular, parents must be informed that:

➤ there is no obligation to take part, and they can withdraw consent at any time, without the child's care being affected

➤ if the research is a clinical trial, the nature of the trial, and the information available so far on the therapy's effectiveness and side-effects

➤ if the research is a randomised controlled trial, the fact that their child will be randomly assigned to the standard treatment, the new treatment or (if applicable) the placebo.

Non-therapeutic research

Non-therapeutic research may arise, where the child will not directly benefit from the proposed intervention. The example given above of taking extra blood samples from a child in order to carry out research related to the condition from which he or she is suffering. Nursing research, involving activities such as interviews with children or asking them to draw pictures, might also come under this category.

Where the child lacks capacity to consent for themselves, those with parental responsibility can consent to a non-therapeutic intervention on a child as long as the intervention is not against the interests of the child and imposes only a minimum burden. 'Minimum burden' should be assessed individually for each child, bearing in mind that children's reactions to injections, for example, vary considerably.

Information should be available for the children involved in research which is easy to understand and they should be encouraged to be involved in any decisions. Where parents have consented to non-therapeutic research, but the child does not agree, the research should not go ahead.

It is always good practice to offer feedback on the results of research to children and parents, to show that you value their participation.

Summary

➤ From birth to 16, consent will come from the parent (or person with parental responsibility) or from the child if they are Gillick competent.

➤ From 16 to 18, two consents are possible – either the parent or the young person.

➤ From 18 years onwards, they are considered an adult and consent will come from them. No one can consent on behalf of an adult.

Case review

Jacqueline is 15 years old. She is suffering from sickle cell anaemia and her treatment requires her to have a blood transfusion. She is refusing to give consent, but her parents are prepared to give consent in her best interests.

1 Would you treat Jacqueline or respect her wishes not to treat her?
2 Would it differ if Jacqueline consented to treatment but her parents refused to consent?
3 Would your view differ if Jacqueline was 16 years old?

Assuming the treatment is not required in an emergency, the following will apply:

1 As Jacqueline is under 16 years old she has no right in law to consent to treatment under the Children Act or the Family Law reform Act. However, she may have the right to consent to treatment if she is considered to be Gillick competent.

   However, Jacqueline is refusing treatment. There is no right in law for Jacqueline to refuse treatment under the Family Law Reform Act or under the Gillick guidelines.

   If Jacqueline's parents consent to her treatment the health professionals could lawfully proceed with treatment.

   However, as Jacqueline is refusing treatment and as it is life saving or because there is a dispute between Jacqueline and her parents it may be appropriate in the circumstances to apply to the court.

2 As Jacqueline consents to treatment but her parents refuse to consent, the treatment may proceed if Jacqueline is Gillick competent as she is 15 years old. Notwithstanding her parents may refuse, Jacqueline can overrule her parent's wishes as it is consent to proceed with treatment, provided she is Gillick competence.

   If Jacqueline is not Gillick competent then there is no valid consent from either Jacqueline or her parents and the health professionals would not be able to proceed with treatment.

   An application to court would be appropriate in the circumstances.

3 If Jacqueline were 16 years old she can consent treatment under the

Family Law Reform Act. If she consents to treatment her parents refusal cannot overrule her decision and the health professionals can lawfully proceed with treatment. However, the Family Law Reform Act does not give her the right to refuse treatment. If Jacqueline refuses treatment her decision can be overruled by her parents or by a court if her parents refuse to give consent on her behalf.

CHECKLIST

Use this checklist as a reminder of matters you need to consider.

Where the child or young person is 16 or 17 years	• Has the child given consent (under the FLRA)? • Have the parents consented to treatment? • Has the child refused treatment? • Is there a dispute between the young person and the parents or health professional? • Is consent capable of being overruled by the child, parent or the court? • Does the court need to be involved? • Is it an emergency?

Where the child is under 16 years	• Have the parents consented to treatment?
	• Is the child Gillick competent?
	• Have the Gillick guidelines been complied with?
	  ‣ Did you seek to persuade the child to involve the parents?
	  ‣ Are you satisfied that the child has sufficient maturity to understand the nature, purpose and likely outcome of the proposed treatment?
	  ‣ Is the proposed treatment in the best interests of the child?
	• Have the parents become involved?
	• Has the child refused treatment?
	• Is it an emergency?

Parental responsibility	• Does the parent or guardian have parental responsibility? • Is the parent under 16 years? • Does the parent have capacity? • Has parental responsibility been delegated? • Is the child a ward of court?
In all cases have you considered the following?	• Is the treatment in the child's best interest? • Is the treatment therapeutic or non-therapeutic? • Is the consent for research or removal of tissue? • Has the child been involved in the consent process? • Who should seek consent?

In all cases have you considered the following? (*cont.*)	• Was consent given voluntary?
	• Have you provided sufficient information?
	• Did those consenting understand?
	• Did those consenting have capacity?
	• Were they given the opportunity to refuse treatment?
	• Were they informed they can refuse or withdraw treatment at any time?
	• Were they informed that they could change their minds at any time whether consent was given or refused?
	• Is there a question of the capacity of the child or person with parental responsibility?
	• Is the child subject to Mental Health legislation
	• Are court proceedings necessary?
	• Does consent cover all procedures including routine procedures?
	• Has it been fully documented?

REFERENCES

1 Inglis R. *Sins of the Fathers: a study of the physical and emotional abuse of children*. London: P Owen; 1978. p. 24.
2 Children Act 1989
3 DHSS. '*A Child in Trust*': *the report of the panel of inquiry into the death of Jasmine Beckford*. London: HMSO; HC Deb 06 May 1986: vol. 97 cc68–9W.
4 Family Procedure (adoption) Rules 2005, Pt 7, r 51
5 Re C (Detention: Medical Treatment) [1997] 2 FLR 180
6 Children Act 1989, s 1
7 Family Law Reform Act 1969, s 8
8 Re W (a minor) (medical treatment) [1992] 4 ALL ER 627
9 Mental Capacity Act 2005
10 Mental Health Act 2007, s 43
11 Re W (a minor) (medical treatment) [1992] 4 ALL ER 627
12 Mental Capacity Act 2005
13 Gillick v West Norfolk and Wisbech AHA and the DHSS [1985] 2 WLR 413
14 Children Act 1989, s 1(3)(a)
15 Gillick v West Norfolk and Wisbech AHA and the DHSS [1985] 2 WLR 413
16 Re R (a minor) Wkly Law Rep. 1991 Jul 11; 1991 Oct 25: 592–608
17 Abortion Act 1967
18 Re W (a minor) (medical treatment) [1992] 4 ALL ER 627
19 *Daily Mail*. 'I didn't want to have any more operations': girl, 13, says why she would prefer to die with dignity than have transplant. 11 November 2008. Available at: www.dailymail. co.uk/news/article-1084531/I-didnt-want-operations-Girl-13-says-prefer-die-dignity-transplant.html (accessed 5 June 2009).
20 Children Act 1989, s 47
21 Children Act 1989, s 20

22 Mental Capacity Act 2005

23 Mental Capacity Act 2005, s 5

24 Mental Capacity Act 2005, s 18(3)

25 Mental Capacity Act 2005, s 44

26 Children Act 1989, s 3(1)

27 Children Act 1989, s 2(1)

28 Children Act 1989, s 2(2)

29 Statutory Instrument 2003 No. 3079 (C.117) Adoption and Children Act 2002 (Commencement No. 4) Order 2003

30 Children Act 1989, s 4(1)(b)

31 Children Act 1989, s 4

32 Human Fertilisation and Embryology Act 1990

33 Children Act 1989, s 2(9)

34 Re J (a child's religious upbringing and circumcision) [2000] 1 FCR 307 CA

35 Department of Health. *Reference Guide to Consent for Examination or Treatment*. London: Department of Health; 2001; British Medical Association. *Withholding and Withdrawing Life Prolonging Medical Treatment: Guidance for Decision-making*. London: BMJ Books; 2001; Royal College of Paediatrics and Child Health. *Withholding or Withdrawing Life-saving Treatment in Children: a framework for practice*. London: Royal College of Paediatrics and Child Health; 1997.

36 Human Tissue Act 2004

37 Human Tissue Act 2004, Sch 1

CHAPTER 12

Consent to video recordings and clinical photography

Conventional or digital video recordings and clinical photography form part of the patient's record. It may be used both as a medical record or treatment aid in themselves, and as a tool for teaching, audit or research. The purpose and possible future use of the video must be clearly explained to the patient before their consent is sought for the recording to be made. If the video is to be used for teaching, audit or research, patients must be aware that they can refuse without their care being compromised and that when required or appropriate the video can be anonymised.

Although consent to certain recordings, such as X-rays, is implicit in the patient's consent to the procedure, health professionals should always ensure that they make clear in advance if any photographic or video recording will result from that procedure.

Photographic and video recordings, which are made for treating or assessing a patient, must not be used for any purpose other than the patient's care or the audit of that care without the express consent of the patient, or a person with parental responsibility for the patient.

If you wish to use such a recording for education publication or research purposes, you must seek consent in writing, ensuring that the person giving consent is fully aware of the possible uses of the material. In particular, the person must be made aware that you may not be able to control future use of the material once it has been placed in the public domain. If a child is not willing for a recording to be used, you must not use it, even if a person with parental responsibility consents. There is an exception to this, photographic and video recordings, made for treating or assessing a patient and from which there is no possibility that the patient might be recognised, may be used within the clinical setting for education or research purposes without express consent from the patient, as long as this policy is well publicised. However, express consent must be sought for any form of publication.

If the health professional wishes to make a photographic and video recording of a patient specifically for education, publication or research purposes, you must first seek their written consent (or where appropriate that of a person with parental responsibility) to make the recording, and then seek their consent to use it. Patients must know that they are free to stop the recording at any time and that they are entitled to view it if they wish, before deciding whether to give consent to its use. If the patient decides they are not happy for any recording to be used, it must be destroyed. As with recordings made with therapeutic intent, patients must receive full information on the possible future users of the recording including the fact that it may not be possible to withdraw it once it is in the public domain. For a patient who lacks capacity *see* Chapter 17.

Video recording for the purpose of covert surveillance is subject to the rules under the Regulation of Investigatory Powers Act 2000 (RIPA).[1] It is not within the ambit of this book.

REFERENCE

1 Regulation of Investigatory Powers Act 2000

CHAPTER 13

Consent and removal of tissue

Tissue left over after routine pathological examination may have a range of potentially beneficial uses, for example, in basic and applied research, in drug testing and in teaching. Further, excess human tissue from medical procedures, such as bone from hip replacements, may have therapeutic uses for others.

In the past, there seems to have been an assumption that such tissue has been abandoned by patients and that it may be freely used for any ethically acceptable purpose without the patient's consent being sought. This assumption was challenged on the basis that patients should be given the opportunity to give or refuse their consent for such use.

The existing law on retention and use of organs and tissue was reviewed following public inquiries into events at Bristol Royal Infirmary[1] and the Royal Liverpool Children's Hospital (Alder Hey).[2] The public inquiry into the Alder Hey hospital revealed the unauthorised removal, retention, and disposal of human tissue. They had over 2000 organs and the number of children involved were more than 850. It prompted the need for regulation. These inquiries, together with the Isaacs Report,[3] which focused on the retention of adult brains following coroners' post mortems, showed that storage and use of organs and tissue without proper consent after people had died were commonplace. The legal review showed that the law on tissue retention, both from the living and the deceased, was inadequate, and that the law on anatomical examination and transplants needed to be updated. The Human Genetics Commission also raised concerns about the scope for DNA 'theft', in cases of disputed paternity, for example.

Following a public consultation, the government decided to update the law in this area to reflect advances in good practice. This was to make it clear that living patients must consent to retention and use of their organs and tissue for particular purposes beyond their diagnosis and treatment. It would also make it clear that there must be consent for removal, retention and use of tissue from people who have died, given either by those people in life, or in the event that they die without expressing a wish, given by someone nominated by, or close to them.

THE HUMAN TISSUE ACT 2004

The Human Tissue Act 2004[4] was implemented in September 2006 and sets out the legal requirement for appropriate consent to remove, store and use human tissue. The Human Tissue Act applies to England, Wales and Northern Ireland. It sets out a legal framework for the storage and use of tissue from the living and for the removal, storage and use of tissue and organs from the dead. This includes 'residual' tissue following clinical and diagnostic procedures.

The Act also established the Human Tissue Authority[5] as the regulatory body for all matters concerning the removal, storage, use and disposal of human tissue (excluding gametes and embryos) for scheduled purposes. This includes responsibility for living donor transplantation. The Act does not deal directly with the removal of tissue from the living. Although the process of seeking consent for the storage and use of tissue from patients will often be undertaken at the same time as consent to investigation or treatment, the consent for removal itself in these circumstances remains a matter of the laws that relate to consent generally.

HUMAN TISSUE AUTHORITY

The Human Tissue Authority sets down a code of practice,[6] which gives practical guidance and lays down the standards expected. It covers consent issues dealing with both the living and the dead.

The Human Tissue Act states that appropriate consent must be obtained from the person concerned, their nominated representative or (in the absence of either of these) the consent of a person in a 'qualifying relationship' with them immediately before they died.

The Human Tissue Act specifies whose consent is needed in all the relevant circumstances but it does not generally give details of when and how consent should be sought, or of what information should be given. The Human Tissue Authority's code provides advice on these issues.

There are different consent requirements which apply when dealing with tissue from the deceased and tissue from the living and from adults and children.

WHEN IS CONSENT REQUIRED?

Consent under the Human Tissue Act relates to the purposes for which material might be removed, stored or used. These purposes are set out in Schedule 1 of the Human Tissue Act[7] and are called scheduled purposes. In broad terms, the Human Tissue Act and the Human Tissue Authority's codes of practice require that consent is required to store and use dead bodies, remove, store and use relevant material from a dead body, store and use relevant material from the living.

Anyone removing, storing or using material in circumstances for which the Act requires consent must be satisfied that consent is in place.

As with the general principles set out in this book for consent to be valid it must be given voluntarily, by an appropriately informed person who has the capacity to agree to the activity in question and so on.

To ensure that the removal, storage or use of any tissue is lawful, it is important to establish clearly that consent has been given. Consent may be expressed in various ways, and does not necessarily need to be in writing. There are exceptions to this which are discussed below.

SCHEDULED PURPOSE

Purposes requiring consent: general

1 Anatomical examination.
2 Determining the cause of death.
3 Establishing, after a person's death, the efficacy of any drug or other treatment administered to him or her.
4 Obtaining scientific or medical information about a living or deceased person which may be relevant to any other person (including a future person).
5 Public display.
6 Research in connection with disorders, or the functioning, of the human body.

7 Transplantation.

Purposes requiring consent: deceased persons
1 Clinical audit.
2 Education or training relating to human health.
3 Performance assessment.
4 Public health monitoring.
5 Quality assurance.

A person's agreement or refusal to consent to the removal, storage or use of tissue for purposes under the Human Tissue Act must not affect the investigation or treatment that they receive.

When is consent required for a scheduled purpose?
Before deciding whether to proceed with the removal, storage or use of tissue for scheduled purposes, the following should be considered.
➤ Does the activity require consent? For tissue from the deceased, consent is required for all scheduled purposes. Consent is not required under the Human Tissue Act for storage and use of tissue from the living in some circumstances
➤ Who may give consent?
➤ Has sufficient written or verbal information been provided for the person giving consent to make a properly considered decision?
➤ How will the consent be given and recorded?
➤ When is written consent required?
➤ Is consent needed for more than one purpose?
➤ If a child is involved, are they competent to consent and have they expressed particular wishes or views?
➤ How does consent apply to adults who lack capacity to consent?
➤ What are the exceptions to the consent provisions?
➤ Is DNA analysis likely to be involved?
➤ What are the consent implications for fetal tissue?

REQUIREMENTS FOR CONSENT FOR THE LIVING
Consent to treatment and examination is covered by the common law and the Mental Capacity Act as set out in this book.

Consent for removal of tissue for a scheduled purpose is covered by the

Human Tissue Act and the Mental Capacity Act. Consent must be obtained from the living for storage and use of tissue for:

➤ obtaining scientific or medical information which may be relevant to any person including a future person
➤ public display
➤ research in connection with disorders, or the functioning, of the human body.

Consent from the living is not needed for storage and use of tissue for:

➤ clinical audit
➤ education or training relating to human health (including training for research into disorders, or the functioning, of the human body)
➤ performance assessment
➤ public health monitoring
➤ quality assurance.

Tissue may be taken in a variety of circumstances, for example:

➤ in the course of diagnostic procedures, e.g. taking a blood or urine sample, tissue biopsy, cervical screening, etc.
➤ in the course of treatment, e.g. removing tissue (organs, tumours, etc.) during surgery
➤ when removed specifically for the purpose of research.

Although consent for treatment and examination is dealt with largely under the common law and consent for scheduled purposes is dealt with under the Human Tissue Act, the consent for each activity may be obtained at the same time. It is still important to explain clearly the activity for which consent is being obtained, including the risks and wider implications.

REQUIREMENTS FOR CONSENT OF THE DECEASED

Under the Human Tissue Act consent is needed for the removal, storage and use of material from the deceased for all scheduled purposes as listed below:

1 anatomical examination
2 determining the cause of death
3 establishing, after a person's death, the efficacy of any drug or other treatment administered to him or her

4 obtaining scientific or medical information, which may be relevant to any person including a future person
5 public display
6 research in connection with disorders, or the functioning, of the human body
7 transplantation
8 clinical audit
9 education or training relating to human health
10 performance assessment
11 public health monitoring and
12 quality assurance.

Does the activity require consent?

When considering removal of tissue health professionals should consider obtaining consent for the specific requirement. Consent is not required under the Human Tissue Act for storage and use of tissue from the living in some circumstances. These circumstances are set out below. Surplus tissue is often an important source of material for research and consent procedures may include an agreement to its use. It is lawful to dispose of surplus tissue. There is a checklist at the end of this chapter.

Multiple Purpose

Healthcare professionals may wish to seek consent for more than one scheduled purpose. For example, if a post-mortem examination is to be carried out, some tissue samples could also usefully be obtained for research purposes. In these circumstances it would be appropriate to seek the relevant consent to both activities. Anticipating and explaining the purpose for which tissue could be used will avoid the need for seeking consent on repeated occasions.

Where consent has been given for the use of tissue or organs after death for transplantation, separate consent is required for its storage and use for research purposes. In such cases, the necessary consents should ideally be sought in a single consent process and recorded in the same place.

In the case of post-mortem tissue, and unless authorised by a coroner, all storage and use for scheduled purposes requires consent. But, if consent to the storage or use of post-mortem samples by whoever originally consented to their storage or use is withdrawn, this must be respected for any samples that are still held. Healthcare professionals should discuss with the person concerned how the samples should be returned to them or disposed of, and tell them about any samples that may have already been used or disposed of.

Who may give consent?
Adults
An adult, while alive, may give consent for any particular donation or the removal, storage or use of their body or tissue for scheduled purposes to take place following their death. As with the general rules of consent the same applies to the removal of tissue. An adult who has capacity can give consent. No one can consent on their behalf. Once consent has been obtained it is lawful to proceed.

Where the patient who has consented dies, those close to the deceased may object to the donation. However, they do not have the legal right to veto or overrule the wishes of the deceased. The healthcare professional should seek to discuss the matter openly and sensitively with them. They should be encouraged to accept the deceased person's wishes and explain to them the legal position. While it is lawful to proceed despite the protest of close family, healthcare professionals may consider that carrying out an anatomical examination would leave relatives or family members traumatised despite the deceased person having consented to this while alive.

Adults who lack capacity to consent
The Human Tissue Act does not specify the criteria for considering whether an adult has capacity to consent. The health professional must consider the requirements under the Mental Capacity Act.[8] The same criteria apply to the removal and retention of tissue as to capacity to consent to medical procedures. Capacity is discussed in detail in Chapter 17.

Nominated representatives
An adult can appoint a person to represent him after his death. This is a 'nominated representative'. The terms may be general or just in relation to consent as they specify in the agreement. It empowers the nominated representative to consent to the removal, storage and use of the body or tissue for any of the scheduled purposes, other than anatomical examination or public display.

If a deceased adult had neither consented to, nor specifically refused, any particular donation or the removal, storage or use of their body or tissue for scheduled purposes, those close to them should be asked whether a nominated representative was appointed to take those decisions.

The appointment of a nominated representative and its terms and conditions may be made orally or in writing. The appointment of a nominated representative may be revoked at any time.

If the deceased person appointed more than one nominated representative, only one of them needs to give consent, unless the terms of the appointment specify that they must act jointly.

The nominated representative's consent cannot be overridden by other individuals, including family members.

Qualifying relationships

If the deceased person has not indicated their consent (or refusal) to post-mortem removal, storage or use of their body or tissue for scheduled purposes, or appointed a nominated representative, then the appropriate consent may be given by someone who was in a 'qualifying relationship'[9] with the deceased person immediately before their death.

Those qualifying are:

➤ a partner – if the two of them (whether of different sexes or the same sex) live as partners in an enduring family relationship
➤ a parent or child (in this context a child may be of any age and means a biological or adopted child)
➤ a brother or sister
➤ a grandparent or grandchild
➤ a niece or nephew
➤ a stepfather or stepmother
➤ a half-brother or half-sister
➤ a friend of long standing.

Consent is needed from only one person in the hierarchy of qualifying relationships and should be obtained from the person ranked highest. If a person high up the list refuses to give consent, it is not possible to act on consent from someone further down the list. For example, if a spouse refuses but others in the family wish to give consent, the wishes of the spouse must be respected.

If there is no one available in a qualifying relationship to make a decision on consent (and consent had not been indicated by the deceased person or a nominated representative), it is not lawful to proceed with removal, storage or use of the deceased person's body or tissue for scheduled purposes.

A person's relationship shall be left out of account if:

➤ they do not wish to deal with the issue of consent

➤ they are not able to deal with the issue in relation to the activity for which consent is sought

➤ it is not practical to communicate with that person within the time available if consent in relation to the activity is to be acted on.

This means a person may be omitted from the hierarchy if they cannot be located in reasonable time for the activity in question to be addressed, declines to deal with the matter or is unable to do so, for example, because they are a child or lack capacity to consent. In such cases, the next person in the hierarchy would become the appropriate person to give consent.

CHILDREN

Children may consent to a proposed medical procedure or the storage and use of their tissue. The general position regarding consent and children is set out in detail in Chapter 11.

A person who was under 18 years of age before they died and was competent to reach a decision and gave consent for one or more scheduled purposes to take place after their death, is the same as that of an adult. Their consent is sufficient to make lawful the removal, storage or use of tissue for that purpose.

If a child consents to a procedure, this consent carries over into adulthood unless they withdraw their consent.

With regard to anatomical examination or public display, written, witnessed consent is required from the child. As with adults, the next of kin cannot agree to the use of a child's body after death for these purposes.

If a child did not make a decision, or was not competent to make a decision, the Human Tissue Act makes clear that the appropriate consent will be that of a person with parental responsibility for the child. Consent of only one person with parental responsibility is necessary. The issue should be discussed fully with relatives and careful thought should be given as to whether to proceed if a disagreement arises between parents or other family members. Any previously stated wishes of the deceased child should be considered, taking into account their age and understanding.

If there is no person with parental responsibility, e.g. if the parents have also died, perhaps at the same time as the child, then consent should be sought from someone in a qualifying relationship. A child cannot appoint nominated representatives and therefore provisions related to seeking consent from nominated representatives do not apply.

HOW LONG DOES CONSENT REGARDING TISSUE LAST?

Consent regarding tissue may have a time limit or may continue until consent is withdrawn. Any time limits should be clearly recorded in the patient's notes, the laboratory records or both.

WITHDRAWAL OF CONSENT

Consent may be withdrawn at any time whether it is generic or specific. Withdrawal should be discussed at the outset when consent is being sought. The practicalities of withdrawing consent and the implications of doing so should be made clear, for example, for potential recipients if the donated tissue is for clinical use. Withdrawal of consent cannot be effective where tissue has already been used.

Where consent is given for their tissue to be stored or used for more than one scheduled purpose and then withdraws consent for a particular scheduled purpose (e.g. research), this does not necessarily mean that the sample or samples have to be removed or destroyed. However, the samples may no longer be stored or used for the particular purpose for which consent has been withdrawn. In addition, if someone withdraws consent for samples to be used in any future projects, this does not mean that information and research data should be withdrawn from any existing projects.

WHEN SHOULD CONSENT BE SOUGHT?

Consent is often sought in a clinical setting for treatment, research, or following the death of a patient. It is good practice to seek the person's consent to the proposed procedure in advance. Sufficient time should be allowed for questions and discussion.

Discussions with families may often take place in hospital before a person's death. They may know the person's wishes in respect of, for example, donating organs for transplantation. It should be made clear to them, however, that knowing and understanding the dying person's wishes is different from consenting on their behalf following their death.

The seeking and obtaining of consent from patients before death or from those close to them after their death requires sensitivity especially for donations for transplantation, post-mortem examinations and the retention of tissue and organs for research.

WHO MAY OBTAIN CONSENT?

As with the general law on consent it is the responsibility of the healthcare professional to seek consent. It may be delegated to someone else provided they know enough about the proposed procedure, the intended use of the tissue and the risks involved, for the subject to make an informed decision. For example, a transplant coordinator or an appropriately trained member of a bereavement services team could be involved in the consent-seeking process. In practice, the deceased person's clinician would usually raise the possibility of a post-mortem examination, knowing the medical problems and the unresolved aspects that merit investigation.

There may be different options for choosing who actually discusses the post mortem and obtains consent, but most will involve a team approach.

Those seeking consent for a hospital post-mortem examination should be sufficiently experienced and well informed, with a thorough knowledge of the procedure. They must be trained in dealing with bereavement, explaining the purpose and procedures and they should have witnessed a post-mortem examination. Those seeking consent may include members of the clinical team involved in the care of the patient before death, and may also include someone closely involved with the pathology department, such as an anatomical pathology technologist (APT) or a specialist nurse.

FORMS OF CONSENT

Consent for anatomical examination or public display of dead bodies or body parts must be in writing and witnessed.

Consent for the retention of tissue for other scheduled purposes is not required in writing although a good record should be made in the notes.

Written consent should be obtained wherever possible for all other post mortem activities. If verbal consent is obtained, this should be clearly documented in the patient's records.

EXAMPLE

A health professional obtains verbal consent over the telephone from the deceased persons' relatives for the donation of eyes and heart valves for transplantation. The family is provided with information about the donation process and the subsequent uses of the tissues. They are given the opportunity to ask questions, to ensure that valid consent is given. The health professional records the details of the discussion, advice and consent in the donor's records. The Human Tissue Authority code also suggests that an audio record of the consent conversation with the family be made if possible, and should be followed up with a letter of confirmation.

Documenting consent and removal of tissue

It is important to document accurately the issues relating to consent and research. This is discussed in details in Chapter 10.

Information

The person giving consent must be provided with sufficient information about the purpose for which consent is being sought in order for them to make a considered decision. This should include: where no decision was made by the deceased; when seeking consent from a nominated representative or from a person in a qualifying relationship, full and clear information should be provided about the purpose for which consent is being sought. This should allow them to make a properly considered decision. This information should include the nature of the intended activities and the reasons for them.

Healthcare professionals need to tailor the information they provide to each specific situation, as some people may insist on in-depth detail, whereas others would prefer to consent having only had the basics of the procedure explained to them. Information may be contained in leaflets or on a consent form. A record of which leaflets have been given should be made in the notes.

It is important to discuss the options with the deceased person's family with sensitivity. They should be given: honest, clear, objective information; the opportunity to talk to someone of whom they feel able to ask questions; reasonable time to reach decisions; privacy for discussion between family members; and support if they need and want it, including the possibility of further advice or psychological support.

Existing tissue held

There is no legal requirement to obtain consent for the storage or use of tissue that is an existing holding. However, this does not mean that all such human tissue can be used freely and without regard to issues of consent or other ethical considerations. If practical, the consent of the participant should be sought and the views of the deceased person or of their family should be respected.

Consent is not required for carrying out research on existing holdings of human tissue and organs. Although existing holdings are exempt from the consent provisions in the Human Tissue Act, the Human Tissue Authority's licensing requirements may still apply where material is being stored or used for a scheduled purpose.

Consent for research purposes

Tissue from the living may be stored or used without consent, provided that

> the researcher is not in possession, and not likely to come into possession of information that identifies the person from whom it has come; and the material is used for a specific research project with ethical approval.[6]

Data about the tissue does not have to be permanently or irrevocably unlinked, and may be pseudonymised where, for example, a system of coding is used.

There may be occasions when a clinician involved in research may also have access to a secure database that would permit identification of a sample used in research and the identity of the patient whose material is being used. Providing the research material is not identifiable to the researcher (e.g. coded by a laboratory accession number) and the researcher does not seek to link the sample to the patient, it will still be regarded as non-identifiable and the research will be permissible without consent if it is given ethical approval by a recognised research ethics committee.

Consent is required to use identifiable patient data in research.[10] Researchers intending to use patient data in research should be aware that such information is subject to the common law duty of confidentiality and the requirements of the Data Protection Act 1998.[11]

Obtaining consent may be preferable to developing complex systems for keeping samples unlinked.

Where identifiable tissue is to be used for research, donors should be informed about any implications this may have. For example, they may be contacted by researchers, given feedback, or be asked for access to their medical records. Donors should be asked whether the consent they are giving is generic, for example for use in any future research project, or specific. Where it is specific detailed information about the research project should be provided.

Those donating tissue should be told if their samples will or could be used for research involving the commercial sector. They should be given appropriate information on the range of activities and researchers which may be involved, and whether these include commercial establishments.

WHEN CONSENT IS NOT REQUIRED

The Human Tissue Act[12] allows the need for consent to be dispensed with for relevant material from someone who is untraceable, or who has not responded to requests for consent to use of their material, if that material could be used to provide information relevant to another person. This may be important where information could be obtained about the treatment and diagnosis of the applicant.

CORONER

Consent is not required for a coroner's post mortem. This is because there is a duty on the coroner to establish the cause of death. The needs of society triumph over individual desires. For example, where there is reason to suspect that a person might well have died of new variant Creutzfeldt-Jakob disease (CJD), the law allows material to be retained from the body without the consent of the next of kin for testing to determine this.

For tissue from the deceased, consent is not needed for carrying out an investigation into the cause of death under the authority of a coroner, retention of material after a post mortem under the authority of a coroner, for a period no longer than the time needed by the coroner to discharge their statutory functions.

However, consent is required for research or other scheduled purposes where the coroner's authority to retain the material has ended and the deceased's family have not opted to dispose of the material. This applies to all tissue removed at post mortem, including small samples such as blocks and slides, and samples that might include relevant material such as toxicology and microbiology specimens.

Once the coroner's authority has ended, if the material is not disposed of, the further storage and use of post-mortem samples fall within the remit of the Human Tissue Act. Once the coroner's authority has ended, it is not lawful to use or store tissue for a scheduled purpose without consent.

CONFIDENTIALITY

A patient is entitled to have information about them be kept confidential, even after death. Care should be taken regarding the possible disclosure of information, such as genetic information or, for example, HIV status, which the deceased person may not have wished to be disclosed, or which may have significant implications for other family members. Healthcare professionals will have to make a decision based on the individual circumstances of each case about whether it is appropriate or not to disclose information about the deceased's medical history, as well as any other sensitive information that the Trust may hold about the deceased, that the family may not necessarily be aware of. In making decisions, healthcare professionals will have to have regard to their duty of patient confidentiality and may have to consider the provisions of the Data Protection Act 1998.[13]

In certain circumstances, it may be necessary to share sensitive information with the family if the results of the activity have the potential to affect them or other relatives. Health professionals must be familiar with the law in relation to confidentiality. Confidentiality is outside the ambit of this book.

TISSUE FOR DNA

Consent is required to analyse DNA, subject to certain exceptions. Where consent to use material has been obtained for a scheduled purpose, it is not necessary to obtain separate consent where that use also involves DNA analysis. However, it should be made clear to the donor that their bodily material may be used for this purpose, if that is the intention. When discussing consent, the donor should be made aware if the intended DNA analysis may reveal significant results, e.g. a family genetic condition. Their decision as to whether they wish such information to be made known to them should be respected in appropriate cases.

It is an offence to hold material with the intent of analysing DNA without consent. However, the offence does not apply if the results of the analysis are intended to be used for 'excepted' purposes.

The following are 'excepted' purposes:

1 medical diagnosis or treatment of that person
2 for the purposes of the coroner
3 prevention or detection of crime or prosecution
4 national security
5 court or tribunal order or direction
6 where the bodily material is from the body of a living person – used for clinical audit, education or training relating to human health, performance assessment, public health monitoring and quality assurance
7 where the bodily material is an existing holding – used for clinical audit, determining the cause of death, education or training relating to human health, establishing after death the efficacy of any drug or treatment administered, obtaining scientific or medical information about a living or deceased person which may be relevant to another person (including a future person), performance assessment, public health monitoring, quality assurance, research in connection with disorders or functioning of the human body and transplantation
8 obtaining scientific or medical information about the person from whose body the DNA has come where the bodily material is the subject of either a direction by the Human Tissue Authority or a court order[14] and the information may be relevant to the person for whose benefit the direction or order is made
9 research in connection with disorders or functioning of the human body, provided the bodily material comes from a living person, the person carrying out the analysis is not in, and not likely to come into, possession of identifying information and the research is ethically approved
10 where the DNA has come from an adult lacking capacity and neither a decision of that person to nor not to consent is in force.

Where an adult dies, a person (such as a relative or friend) who was close to them at the point of death, may give consent for a DNA test. Usually this operates on a hierarchical basis[15] but in cases relating to DNA analysis, this ranking does not apply. The person giving consent should, however, be encouraged to discuss the decision with other family members. At the time of discussing consent, it should be raised with the family whether they wish to know of any results that may have potential significance such as a genetic condition.

In exceptional circumstances, DNA analysis may be used for obtaining scientific or medical information about the person whose body manufactured the DNA, even if their consent has not been obtained.

The Human Tissue Authority[16] can direct the use of DNA without consent if it is satisfied that:

➤ It is 'not reasonably possible to trace the person'[17] or
➤ 'reasonable efforts have been made to get the donor to decide'.[18]

FETAL TISSUE

The law does not distinguish between fetal tissue and other tissue from the living. Fetal tissue is regarded as the mother's tissue. Fetal tissue is therefore subject to the same consent requirements under the Human Tissue Act as all other tissue from the living. However, because of the sensitivity attached to this subject, it is good practice to always obtain consent for the examination of fetal tissue and for its storage or use for all scheduled purposes. It is also good practice to obtain consent for research on non-fetal products of conception for example, placenta, membranes, umbilical cord, or amniotic fluid, even where the tissue is non-identifiable.

Fetal tissue does not include stillbirths (babies born dead after 24 weeks gestation), or neonatal deaths (babies or fetuses of any gestational age which are born showing signs of life and die before the age of 28 days). Obtaining consent for the removal, storage or use of the tissue of babies from stillbirths or neonatal deaths should be handled in accordance with provisions for gaining consent for use of the tissue of the deceased.

It is recommended that, whenever possible, the consent process for the examination of stillbirths and neonatal deaths involves the mother, and that, where appropriate, both parents are involved.

There are no specific legal requirements on the use of fetuses and fetal tissue for research. Therefore guidance has been derived from the 1989 *Review of the Guidance on the Research Use of Fetuses and Fetal Material*,[19] also known as the Polkinghorne guidelines. A number of aspects of the Polkinghorne guidelines are outside the remit of the Human Tissue Act and the Human Tissue Authority code of practice. However, it should be noted that guidance within the Polkinghorne guidelines which recommended that in the context of giving consent, women should not know the purpose for which the fetus would be used, or whether it would be used at all, is now superseded by guidance within the Human Tissue Authority Code on valid consent, which must be based on the person's understanding of what the activity involves.

CHECKLIST

Human tissue

Scheduled purpose	Consent required for human tissue from the living			Consent required for human tissue from the deceased		
	Removal	Storage	Use	Removal	Storage	Use
Anatomical examination	N/A	N/A	N/A	✓	✓	✓
Determining cause of death	N/A	N/A	N/A	✓	✓	✓
Establishing after a person's death the efficacy of any drug or other treatment administered to him or her	N/A	N/A	N/A	✓	✓	✓
Obtaining scientific or medical information about a living or deceased person which may be relevant to any other person	✗ *	✓	✓	✓	✓	✓
Public display	✗ *	✓	✓	✓	✓	✓
Research in connection with disorders, or functioning of the human body	✗ *	✓	✓	✓	✓	✓
Transplantation	✗ *	✓	✓	✓	✓	✓
Clinical audit	✗ *	✗	✗	✓	✓	✓
Education and training	✗ *	✗	✗	✓	✓	✓
Performance assessment	✗ *	✗	✗	✓	✓	✓
Public health monitoring	✗ *	✗	✗	✓	✓	✓
Quality assurance	✗ *	✗	✗	✓	✓	✓

✓ Consent is required under the Human Tissue Act
✗ Consent is not required under the Human Tissue Act
* Consent is required under the common law for the removal of tissue in the living

The checklist sets out the legal requirement as to when consent is required. However, the Human Tissue Authority sets down a code where it is also good practice to obtain consent.

REFERENCES

1 Bristol Royal Infirmary. *Learning from Bristol: the report into children's heart surgery at Bristol Royal Infirmary 1984–1995*. London: Department of Health; July 2001.

2 Redfern M, QC, Keeling J. *The Royal Liverpool Children's Hospital Inquiry Report*. London: Stationery Office; January 2001: HC12-II.

3 Department of Health. *Isaacs Report: the investigation of events that followed the death of Cyril Mark Isaacs*. London: Stationery Office; May 2003; Department of Health. *Isaacs Report Response: response to the report by Her Majesty's Inspector of Anatomy*. London: Department of Health; July 2003.

4 The Human Tissue Act 2004 (the Human Tissue Act 2006 applies to Scotland and is not within the ambit of this book).

5 Human Tissue Authority. Available at: www.hta.gov.uk/ (accessed 9 October 2009).

6 *The Human Tissue Authority Code of Practice 2009*. Available at: www.hta.gov.uk/legislationpoliciesandcodesofpractice/codesofpractice/code1consent.cfm (accessed 11 July 2010).

7 Human Tissue Act 2004, Sch 1

8 Mental Capacity Act 2005

9 Human Tissue Act 2004, s 27(4)

10 In cases where researchers do not have consent to use identifiable patient data for research, they should refer to the National Information Governance Board for Health and Social Care (NIGB). Available at: www.nigb.nhs.uk/ (accessed 27 July 2010).

11 Data Protection Act 1998

12 The Human Tissue Act 2004, ss 7 and 12

13 Data Protection Act 1998.

14 Human Tissue Act 2004, Sch 4, s 9

15 Human Tissue Act 2004, s 27(4)

16 Human Tissue Act 2004, Sch 4, s 9(2) and (3)

17 Human Tissue Act 2004, Sch 4, s 9(2)

18 Human Tissue Act 2004, Sch 4, s 9(3)

19 Polkinghorne J. *Review of the Guidance on the Research Use of Fetuses and Fetal Material* [Polkinghorne Guidelines or Report]. London: HMSO; 1989.

CHAPTER 14

Research and innovative treatment

The purpose of research is to gain knowledge and understanding through original investigation. Health professionals have an increasingly active role in research in order to develop new knowledge and to create a larger evidence base to inform their practice. This involves health professionals developing protocols, leading investigations and collaborating with colleagues from other disciplines and institutions.

All research proposals should be subject to independent scrutiny to ensure they are ethically acceptable. The application for ethical approval will include details of the proposed processes for gaining informed consent.

The same legal principles apply when seeking consent from patients for research purposes as when seeking consent for investigations or treatment. Obtaining consent from research participants is a vital part of the research process. In acknowledgement of the fact that research may not have direct benefits for the patients involved particular care should be taken to ensure that possible research subjects have the fullest possible information about the proposed study and sufficient time to absorb it. Patients should never feel pressurised to take part, and advice must be given that they can withdraw from the research project at any time, without their care being affected. If patients are being offered the opportunity to participate in a clinical trial, they should have clear information on the nature of the trial.

If the treatment being offered is of an experimental nature, but not actually part of a research trial, this fact must be clearly explained to patients before their consent is sought, along with information about standard alternatives. It is good practice to give patients information about the evidence to date of the effectiveness of the new treatment, both at national/international level and in the practitioner's own experience, including information about known possible side-effects.

Where patients are being offered the opportunity to participate in a clinical trial, they should have clear information on the nature of the trial. They should be informed of the following:

➤ purpose of the research
➤ practicalities and procedures involved in participating
➤ benefits and risks of participation and, if appropriate, the alternative therapies
➤ how data about them will be managed and used
➤ the consent form
➤ their role if they agree to participate in the research
➤ how information will be provided to them throughout the study
➤ their participation is voluntary
➤ they can withdraw from the study at any time, without giving any reason and without compromising their future treatment
➤ the insurance indemnity arrangements for the conduct of the research where appropriate
➤ that the research has been approved by a research ethics committee.

They should also be given the following information:
➤ contact details, should they have further questions or wish to withdraw
➤ details of the research sponsor and research funding body.

Remember consent must be voluntary. Patients should never feel pressurised to take part, and advice must be given that they can withdraw from the research project at any time, without their care being affected.

Consent is a requirement where research involves an invasive procedure. If a research activity proceeds without an individual's consent legal action could be taken against the chief investigator or researcher for battery.

Where treatment being offered is of an experimental nature, but not actually part of a research trial, this fact must be clearly explained to patients before their consent is sought, together with information about alternatives. It is good practice to give patients information about the evidence to date of the effectiveness of the new treatment, both at national and international level and in the practitioner's own experience, including information about known possible side-effects.

Consent is an ongoing requirement. Throughout the study researchers must ensure that participants continue to understand the information and must inform them of any changes in that information for valid consent to continue.

SPECIAL CIRCUMSTANCES

It is not always possible to obtain participants' consent before research activity begins. This should not prevent important research from being undertaken, but researchers must take great care to protect the interests of participants and to consult other appropriate people about an individual's participation.

DELAYED CONSENT

Occasionally, consent may be delayed in an emergency situation when obtaining informed consent might make the study impossible. For example, delayed consent may be needed for research undertaken at the roadside of an accident, at a cardiac arrest or during the early stages of a patient's emergency admission to an accident and emergency department.

The Mental Capacity Act 2005[1] states that urgent or emergency research can be undertaken if 'it is not reasonably practical' to meet the requirements for informed consent from a potential participant who lacks the capacity to consent for themselves. The research team will be expected to demonstrate to an ethics committee that this research is necessary and could not have been undertaken in a population where participants were able to provide informed consent in advance. In each instance, the research team should seek informed consent as soon as possible from the participant. Capacity is discussed in more detail in Chapter 17.

IMPLIED CONSENT TO RESEARCH

Consent to research may be implied where, for example, a participant returns a completed anonymous questionnaire. In other situations, potential participants with severe disabilities or multiple injuries may be unable to communicate their consent verbally or in writing. In these cases, researchers can gain implied consent, in which a person indicates consent by their actions after they have received information about the study. In such circumstances a protocol should require that a witness is present who also signs the consent form.

A researcher or a witness can infer that a patient has given implied consent when each of these criteria are met:

➤ the patient can reasonably be expected to be aware of the sharing of their data and to understand the need for it to be shared

➤ the benefits to the patient or the public outweigh the risks to the patient

➤ the patient is offered a clear procedure for withholding consent, but does not do so.

RESPONSIBILITY

Overall responsibility for all elements of research activity, including gaining consent, rests with the lead researcher, although each individual member of the research team is responsible for their own specific actions. The lead researcher may delegate the task of obtaining informed consent to another appropriately qualified member of the research team, but this delegation must be clearly documented, and the person gaining informed consent must sign the consent form when required. To sign a consent form when they have not personally been involved is fraudulent.

Where health professionals are not leading research studies they may nevertheless be involved in delivering the intervention concerned. In these circumstances health professionals are accountable for their own practice. Whatever the level of involvement, health professionals must be satisfied that participants have given informed consent to take part in the research study before they act.

RESEARCH PARTICIPANTS

Potential participants may be unable or unwilling to cooperate with the researcher in these circumstances they should consider withdrawing from the research. They should be informed that withdrawal from a clinical study will not compromise the quality of care they receive, although their treatment may change. For example, if the study is examining a new treatment, they may go back to receiving standard treatment.

There may be benefits to the patient in participating in research. This may influence their decision to participate. Benefits may include:

➤ access to experimental treatments that might give better outcomes than standard treatments
➤ closer monitoring
➤ increased access to members of the multidisciplinary team
➤ extra investigations
➤ the satisfaction of benefiting future patients
➤ financial benefits such as payment to participate, travel costs, child care costs and time off work.

Patients must not be coerced by offering benefits as this will invalidate consent. If the proposed study is a randomised controlled trial, it should be made clear that potential participants might not receive the experimental treatment or an intervention but may receive standard care or a placebo.

Patients must be given sufficient detail to inform them so they may decide for themselves whether to take part in research. They must not be influenced and health professionals must not impose their own value judgments.

HUMAN TISSUE AND RESEARCH

Human tissue and research is dealt with in Chapter 13. Where identifiable tissue is to be used for research, donors should be informed about any implications this may have. For example, they may be contacted by researchers, given feedback, or be asked for access to their medical records. Donors should be asked whether the consent they are giving is generic, for example for use in any future research project, or specific. Where it is specific detailed information about the research project should be provided.

Those donating tissue should be told if their samples will or could be used for research involving the commercial sector. They should be given appropriate information on the range of activities and researchers which may be involved, and whether these include commercial establishments.

RESEARCH BEST INTEREST

Health professionals are accountable for practice and should always act in the best interest of their patient. The key principle in obtaining informed consent in research is to put the potential participant's needs first. To participate effectively in consent processes, health professionals should have the knowledge, expertise and skill to give sufficient information and be able to answer any questions raised by a potential research participant. Health professionals should be open and honest, and ensure the participant understands all they need to about the study. They should be told that they may withdraw from the study at any time and that this will not affect their treatment or care.

Research and adults who lack capacity is dealt with in Chapter 17.

Children and research is dealt with in Chapter 11.

INNOVATIVE NATURE

If the treatment being offered is of an experimental nature, but not actually part of a research trial, this fact must be clearly explained to patients before their consent is sought, along with information about standard alternatives. It is good practice to give patients information about the evidence to date of the effectiveness of the new treatment, both at national and international level and in the practitioner's own experience, including information about known possible side-effects.

CASE

JS v An NHS Trust and JA v An NHS Trust 2002[2]

This case concerned two young people, JS, a boy of 18 years of age, and JA a girl aged 16. Both were suffering from variant Creutzfeldt-Jakob disease (vCJD). In each case their parents sought a declaration from the Court that JS and JA lacked the capacity to make a decision about future treatment proposed for them and that it was lawful as being in their best interests for them to receive it. The proposed treatment was new and untested on human beings.

The enjoyment of the lives of both JA and JS were severely limited. Both families considered that it was in the best interests of JS and JA for them to be given this treatment and they would be content if the proposed treatment only prolonged their life in their present conditions and slowed the course of the disease. Evidence from those who were nursing the patients gave evidence that extending their survival was worthwhile, despite their severe neurological impairment.

The treatment had never been tried on humans and several doctors gave evidence. Dr T identified that there was a risk of intra-cranial haemorrhage which could range from mild to extreme. The risk of this occurrence was a maximum of 5%. Dr K stated he could not, on balance, see grounds for denying

---

JS and JA as there was a theoretical chance of success. He was aware of his duty not to cause undue suffering to a patient and acknowledged that the risk of haemorrhage and the toxic nature the treatment need to be balanced against the uncertainty of success. The progressive and fatal nature of the disease tipped the balance in favour of treatment and he agreed to administer the treatment. Professor W, however, was of the opinion that even if the treatment were effective, it would be unlikely that there would be evidence of neurological improvement. The treatment would involve discomfort, possible distress and might only prolong survival without any clinical improvements. The likely benefits were speculative and there were clearly risks. He did not believe that the benefits outweighed the risks and did not believe the treatment was in the best interests of the patients.

Both sets of parents gave evidence that if either JS or JA had retained capacity, they would have been likely to have chosen for themselves to try this proposed treatment. It was agreed by the consultants from whom the courts sought opinions, that neither JS nor JA was competent to make decisions about the proposed treatment.

The court held that the first duty of a doctor in the case of an incapacitated patient when making a decision about treatment was to ensure he was acting in accordance with a responsible and competent body of medical opinion under the Bolam test. The second duty was to act in the best interests of the mentally incapacitated patient. The court was satisfied that the proposed treatment was consistent with the philosophy underpinning the Bolam test, i.e. there was a responsible body of medical opinion which supported the innovative treatment. Furthermore, it was reasonable to consider experimental treatment with unknown benefits and risks where there was some chance of benefit to the patient. A patient ought not to be deprived of such a chance where it is likely that he would have consented had he been competent. The court held therefore that the treatment complied with the Bolam test. It was also in JA and JS's best interests to have the treatment as there were potential benefits that might otherwise not be afforded to them, notwithstanding the chance of improvement was only slight. Both patients had little to lose by going ahead with the treatment. The court made a declaration that it would be lawful and in the patients' best interests for the treatment to be carried out.

After judgment was given the court was informed that the Hospital Trust's Clinical Governance and Quality Committee had since met and decided it was unable to approve the treatment. The court expressed the view that it was unsatisfactory that a hospital Trust providing innovative treatment to its patients, had not formed its own conclusions in relation to the treatment before the court made its decision. The judge emphasised that while a declaration as to what is lawful is sufficient clarification of the legal position, it does not constitute a mandatory order, and no court could force medical professionals to give the treatment.

REFERENCES

1 Mental Capacity Act 2005
2 JS (Official Solicitor acting as litigation friend) v An NHS Trust and JA v An NHS Trust (Official Solicitor acting as Guardian ad Litem) [2002] EWHC 2734 (Fam)

CHAPTER 15

Withholding and withdrawing treatment

The same legal principles apply to withdrawing and withholding life-prolonging treatment as apply to any other medical intervention.

Healthcare professionals owe a duty of care to their patients and to take reasonable steps to prolong their life. Although there is a strong presumption in favour of providing life-sustaining treatment, there are circumstances when continuing or providing life-sustaining treatment stops providing a benefit to a patient and is not clinically indicated. Health professionals must always act in the best interests of their patients. The gravity and sensitivity of decisions concerning life-prolonging treatment are such that the assessment of capacity and of best interests are particularly important.

Benefits and burdens for the patient are not always limited to purely medical considerations, and health professionals should be careful, particularly when dealing with patients who cannot make decisions for themselves, to take account of all the other factors relevant to the circumstances of the particular patient. It may be very difficult to arrive at a view about the preferences of patients who cannot decide for themselves, and health professionals must not simply substitute their own values or those of the people consulted and must not be motivated by a desire to bring about the person's death.[1]

Life has a natural end and health professionals should recognise that the point may come in the progression of a patient's condition where death is drawing near. In these circumstances health professionals should not strive to prolong the dying process with no regard to the patient's wishes, where known, or an up-to-date assessment of the benefits and burdens of treatment or non-treatment.

There is an important distinction between withdrawing or withholding treatment which is of no clinical benefit to the patient or is not in the patient's best interests, and taking a deliberate action to end the patient's life. A deliberate action which is intended to cause death is unlawful and constitutes a criminal offence of murder or manslaughter.

ADULT PATIENTS WHO CAN CONSENT FOR THEMSELVES

As mentioned earlier the legal principles of consent apply to all medical interventions including withholding and withdrawing treatment. A competent adult therefore has the right to consent to or refuse treatment even where refusal may result in harm to themselves or in their own death. A patient may reach a stage where they no longer wish treatment to continue. Health professionals must respect the patient's wishes.

A competent adult can express their wishes about future treatment in advance. Any valid advance refusal of treatment, one made when the patient was competent and on the basis of adequate information about the implications of their choice, is legally binding and must be respected where it is clearly applicable to the patient's present circumstances and where there is no reason to believe that the patient had changed their mind. Refusal of treatment is discussed further in Chapter 6.

Although there is a strong presumption in favour of providing life-sustaining treatment, there are circumstances when continuing or providing life-sustaining treatment stops providing a benefit to a patient and is not clinically indicated. Healthcare professionals should discuss the situation with a patient with capacity and agree if and when the patient no longer wishes treatment to continue. Suitable care should be provided to ensure that both the comfort and dignity of the patient are maintained.

ADULT PATIENTS WHO CANNOT CONSENT FOR THEMSELVES

Where adults lack capacity to decide for themselves about life-prolonging treatment, health professionals must apply the Mental Capacity Act 2005.[2] The dying process itself may affect a patient's capacity. If a patient lacks capacity, decisions about their life-prolonging treatment must be taken in their best interests and in a way that reflects their wishes, if these are known. Before deciding to withdraw or withhold life-sustaining treatment, the healthcare professional must consider the range of treatment options available in order to work out what would be in the person's best interests.

All of the factors set out in the Mental Capacity Act 2005[3] and Code of Practice should be considered. In particular, the healthcare professional should consider any statements that the person has previously made about their wishes and feelings about life-sustaining treatment and must have regard to any advance instructions that were made at a time when the patient had capacity. Healthcare professionals should also refer to relevant professional guidance when making decisions regarding life-sustaining treatment.

Health professionals must assess capacity and must document it in detail. Capacity is discussed in more detail in Chapter 17.

WITHDRAWING OR WITHHOLDING ARTIFICIAL NUTRITION AND HYDRATION (ANH)

The use of artificial nutrition and hydration (ANH) constitutes medical treatment. The legal principles which apply to the use of ANH are the same as those which apply to all other medical treatments.

Where a patient indicated while they had capacity, their wish to be kept alive by the provision of ANH, the health professionals' duty of care requires the provision of ANH while this treatment continues to prolong life. Where life depends upon the continued provision of ANH, then it will be clinically indicated.

If the patient lacks capacity, all reasonable steps that are in the person's best interests should be taken to prolong their life.

Although there is a strong presumption in favour of providing life-sustaining treatment, there are circumstances when continuing or providing life-sustaining treatment stops providing a benefit to a patient and is not clinically indicated.[4]

BURKE v GMC[5]

Mr Burke sought a declaration from the court. He was suffering from cerebellar ataxia, a progressive degenerative disease, which would eventually lead to loss of speech and movement and would require treatment by way of artificial nutrition and hydration to keep him alive. He was concerned when, if at all, such treatment could be lawfully withdrawn. He was afraid that when he became unable to communicate, although he may still be conscious of what was happening to him, artificial feeding would be withdrawn with the effect that he would be aware of being starved to death. He found such a prospect frightening. Accordingly, Mr Burke wanted to be sure that doctors would not, contrary to his wishes, be able to withdraw feeding. Mr Burke argued that existing guidance issued by the General Medical Council was unlawful in so far as it failed to protect the rights of a patient expressing an advance directive to carry on life-prolonging treatment.

He relied on principles of common law and on Articles 2 and 3 of the European Convention on Human Rights dealing respectively with the 'right to life' and the 'prohibition against inhumane and degrading treatment'.

The Court concluded that an adult patient with capacity does not have the legal right to demand treatment that is not clinically indicated. Where a patient with capacity indicates their wish to be kept alive by the provision of ANH, the health professionals duty of care will require them to provide ANH while such treatment continues to prolong life. A patient cannot demand that a healthcare professional do something unlawful such as assisting them to commit suicide.

Decisions about the proposed withholding or withdrawal of artificial nutrition and hydration from a patient in a permanent vegetative state should be referred to court.[3]

CHILDREN WHO CAN CONSENT

If a child with capacity refuses life-prolonging treatment it is possible that such a refusal could be overruled if it would in all probability lead to the death of the child or to severe permanent injury. The courts consider that to take a decision which may result in the individual's death requires a very high level of understanding, so that many young people who would have the capacity to take other decisions about their medical care would lack the capacity to make such a grave decision.

Refusal of treatment by a child with capacity must always be taken very seriously, even though legally it is possible to override their objections. It is not a legal requirement to continue a child's life-sustaining treatment in all circumstances. For example, where the child is suffering an illness where the likelihood of survival even with treatment is extremely poor, and treatment will pose a significant burden to the child, it may not be in the best interests of the child to continue treatment.

CHILDREN WHO CANNOT CONSENT

Where a child lacks capacity, it is still good practice to involve the child as far as is possible and appropriate in the decision. The decision to withdraw or withhold life-sustaining treatment must be made in the best interests of the child. The best interests of a child in the context of the withholding of medical treatment should be interpreted more broadly than medical interests, and should include emotional and other factors. While there is a strong presumption in favour of preserving life, there is no obligation on healthcare professionals to give treatment that would be futile. If there is disagreement between those with parental responsibility for the child and the clinical team concerning the appropriate course of action, a ruling should be sought from the court as early as possible. This requirement was emphasised in the case of Glass.[6]

CASE

Glass v United Kingdom[7]

David Glass was born in 1986 suffering from a serious neurological disability. In July 1998, David developed respiratory distress, and was taken into hospital. After 23 days, he was put on a ventilator, but soon removed from it, as doctors said he was dying. His mother, Carol, asked for David to be put back on the ventilator. David rallied, and was sent home and readmitted several times, each time becoming more ill.

On 20 October 1998, doctors suggested putting David on diamorphine to alleviate terminal distress and marked his health records 'not for resuscitation'. Carol refused the treatment of diamorphine and asked for David to be resuscitated if he stopped breathing. The doctors insisted that David be given diamorphine, saying that if Carol took him out of the hospital, she would be arrested and a child protection order put on David. A diamorphine drip was set up with the aim of letting David die with dignity.

The family watched him turn blue and lapse into a coma. Carol said that if David were really dying, she would like to take him home. A policewoman, who had been called by the hospital told her that if she attempted to remove David from the hospital, she would be arrested.

Carol's family took matters into their own hands and desperately tried to resuscitate David. Their actions caused a confrontation with the doctors who still refused to stop the diamorphine, saying there was nothing more that could

---

be done and that 'nature should be allowed to take its course'. A disturbance broke out between the family and doctors who were, allegedly, attacked as the family tried to save David's life.

Later that night, the hospital said they did not want to treat David anymore and told Carol to take him home. Under the care of her family and the GP David improved.

The European Court of Human Rights held that a decision of health professionals to override the wishes of the mother of a seriously ill child gave rise to a breach of Article 8 of the European Convention on Human Rights. The court was critical of the fact that the courts were not involved at an earlier stage, and held that, in the event of a continued disagreement between parents and doctors about a child's treatment, the courts should be consulted, and particularly before the matter reaches an emergency situation.

A person with parental responsibility for a child or young person can consent to treatment on their behalf. A person with parental responsibility cannot demand a particular treatment to be continued where the burdens of the treatment clearly outweigh the benefits for the child. If agreement cannot be reached between the parents and the healthcare professionals, a court should be asked to make a declaration about whether the provision of life-sustaining treatment would benefit the child. In exceptional cases, the court has been willing to authorise the withdrawal of life-sustaining treatment against the parents' wishes. However, the views of the parents are given great weight by the courts and are usually determinative unless they conflict with the child's best interests.[8]

WITHHOLDING LIFE-PROLONGING TREATMENT IN AN EMERGENCY

There will be occasions when decisions will need to be made immediately in circumstances where the outcome of treatment is unclear, such as patients who require intensive care or resuscitation following trauma and the wishes of the patient is unknown. In these circumstances providing life-sustaining treatment would be regarded as being in the patient's best interests.

When more time is available and the patient lacks capacity, all those concerned with the care of the patient, such as relatives, partners, friends, carers and the multidisciplinary team, can potentially make a contribution to the assessment. The discussions and the basis for decisions should be recorded in the notes.

REFERENCES

1 Mental Capacity Act 2005, s 4(5)
2 Mental Capacity Act 2005
3 Mental Capacity Act 2005
4 Burke v the General Medical Council [2005] 3 WLR 1132
5 Burke v the General Medical Council [2005] 3 WLR 1132
6 Glass v United Kingdom (61827/00) [2004] 1 FLR 1019 European Court of Human Rights
7 Glass v United Kingdom (61827/00) [2004] 1 FLR 1019 European Court of Human Rights
8 Re C (a minor) (medical treatment) [1998] 1 FLR 384; 6 [2000] 2 FLR 677

CHAPTER 16

Acting in an emergency

There are many circumstances when a health professional is presented with an emergency situation, for example a patient brought into accident and emergency following a road traffic accident or heart attack or during an operation when something unexpected and life threatening occurs.

Questions

In these situations where the patient is unconscious or unable to communicate, how does the health professional obtain consent to treat them?

What if the health professional proceeds with treatment without obtaining consent?

When a health professional has to act in a situation where an emergency arises and it is not possible to find out a patient's wishes, the health professional can treat the patient without their consent, provided the treatment is immediately necessary to save their life or to prevent a serious deterioration of their condition. The treatment provided must be the least restrictive of the patient's future choices. For as long as the patient lacks capacity, ongoing care should be provided.

If the patient regains capacity they should be told what has been done, and why, as soon as they are sufficiently recovered to understand.

In these circumstances the patient is being treated without valid consent. However, because the health professional is acting in an emergency in order to save their life, this is a defence.

THE UNCONSCIOUS PATIENT

> ### EXAMPLE
>
> John is brought into the emergency department following a road traffic acci-
> dent. He is unconscious. He has life-threatening injuries and the trauma team
> say he needs emergency surgery to save his life. John is unknown to the hos-
> pital, they have no records and the family have not yet been tracked down by
> the police to inform them. They have no more information.

When a patient is unconscious and it is not therefore possible to obtain their consent or establish their wishes, they may be treated if it is an emergency to save their life or to prevent a serious deterioration of their condition. The health professional must take into account any advance statement as to their wishes.

> ### EXAMPLE
>
> Freda is undergoing heart surgery. Her consent has been obtained for the
> operation. It is likely that she will be in intensive care for a few days following
> surgery. Freda suffered internal bleeding and further surgery was required.
> Further care and procedures are usually undertaken following this surgery
> although no consent was obtained for further care or treatment.

A patient may be unconscious following surgery which was anticipated or planned. In these circumstances it would have been prudent to obtain consent for any anticipated procedures or care prior to surgery taking place. This is discussed in more detail in Chapter 9 under 'Additional procedures'.

If the treatment or care can wait until the patient regains consciousness, the treatment should not proceed and consent of the patient should be sought once the patient has regained consciousness. The health professional should only carry out necessary care or treatment until the patient's capacity returns.

When a patient is unconscious, the health professional should consider:
➤ whether the patient's lack of capacity is temporary or permanent
➤ which options for treatment would provide overall clinical benefit for
   the patient

➤ which option, including the option not to treat, would be least restrictive of the patient's future choices
➤ any evidence of the patient's previously expressed preferences such as:
  • an advance statement or decision
  • the views of anyone the patient asks you to consult, or who has legal authority to make a decision on their behalf, or has been appointed to represent them
  • the views of people close to the patient on the patient's preferences, feelings, beliefs and values, and whether they consider the proposed treatment to be in the patient's best interests
  • what the health professional and the healthcare team know about the patient's wishes, feelings, beliefs and values.

Whenever the issue of capacity arises health professionals must adhere to the provisions of the Mental Capacity Act 2005 (MCA).[1] The MCA and the issues of capacity are discussed in more detail in Chapter 17.

REFERENCE
1 Mental Capacity Act 2005

Capacity

INTRODUCTION TO CAPACITY AND CONSENT

The general principle of consent is that an adult can consent for themselves and no one else can consent on their behalf. The difficulty for health professionals is when there is question over their capacity, how to determine if someone lacks capacity and in such circumstances what steps can be taken to treat them.

When a patient refuses treatment that would otherwise save their life, there can be a temptation by a health professional to render them lacking capacity as no right-thinking person would make that decision and therefore they must lack capacity! This view is not upheld by the law.

It is not appropriate for health professionals to wait for a patient to become incapacitated so that treatment can proceed against the wishes of the patient. For example, where a woman refuses a caesarean section, you cannot wait until she passes out and then say, 'she now lacks capacity therefore we can treat her'!

Capacity should not be confused with a health professional's assessment of the reasonableness of the patient's decision. The patient is entitled to make a decision which is based on their own religious belief or value system, even if it is perceived by others to be irrational, as long as the patient understands what is entailed in their decision. An irrational decision has been defined as one which is so outrageous in its defiance of logic or of accepted moral standards that no sensible person who had applied his or her mind to the question could have arrived at it.

However, if the decision which appears irrational is based on a misperception of reality, as opposed to an unusual value system – for example, a patient who, despite the obvious evidence, denies that his foot is gangrenous, or a patient with anorexia nervosa who is unable to comprehend her failing physical condition – then the patient may not be able to comprehend and make use of the relevant information and hence may lack capacity to make the decision in question.

In practice, patients also need to be able to communicate their decision. Care should be taken not to underestimate the ability of a patient to communicate, whatever their condition. Health professionals should take all steps which are reasonable in the circumstances to facilitate communication with the patient, using interpreters or communication aids as appropriate.

Care should also be taken not to underestimate the capacity of a patient with a learning disability to understand. Many people with learning disabilities have the capacity to consent if time is spent explaining to the individual the issues in simple language, using visual aids and signing if necessary.

Where appropriate, those who know the patient well, including their family, carers and staff from professional or voluntary support services, may be able to advise on the best ways to communicate with the person.

Where a health professional believes there is a question over the patients' capacity to consent to treatment they must have regard to the law that applies to capacity. The law that applies to capacity is the Mental Capacity Act 2005[1] and the Code of Practice.[2] The Mental Health Act 1983 (MHA)[3] and Mental Health Act 2007[4] also impacts on capacity. The MHA will be dealt with separately later in this chapter.

In a nutshell, where a person's capacity is in question the MCA and the Code of Practice applies. Where someone does lack capacity the MCA sets out circumstances in which it will be lawful to carry out such examinations or treatment without consent. Treatment includes day-to-day care such as feeding and bathing.

Health professionals must keep a record of all assessments and decisions they have made.

These issues are explained in more detail below.

THE MENTAL CAPACITY ACT 2005 (MCA)

The law relating to capacity is governed by the Mental Capacity Act 2005 (MCA) and the Code of Practice. The MCA was fully implemented in

October 2007 and applies to England and Wales. Further guidance on the Lasting Power of Attorney was published in July 2009.[5] Health professionals have an obligation to keep abreast of the law in this area as it effects them and they should keep an eye on any further developments in respect of capacity as it is still evolving.

The Code of Practice

The Code has an important role in the operation of the MCA and needs to be consulted by everyone involved in the care of people who may lack capacity to make decisions. The Code of Practice provides guidance on the operation of the MCA and best practice and should be followed in order to justify the actions and interventions of the health professional.

The Minister of State for Health Services (March 2006) said that:

'the Code of Practice will ensure that best practice is followed and strict safeguards are in place to protect these most vulnerable people.'

The purpose of the MCA

The MCA brought together common law and other existing legal requirements to provide consistency in decision-making about the care and treatment of people who lack capacity to make a decision. It also introduced new criminal offences, independent mental capacity advocates (IMCAs), a new Court of Protection and the Office of the Public Guardian.

The MCA was designed to protect the rights of individuals and to empower vulnerable adults. In the past, some people with dementia, learning disabilities and severe mental illness have often not been listened to, and their rights to make decisions may not have been recognised.

The MCA covers decisions that range from day-to-day decisions such as what to eat and wear, through to serious decisions about where to live.

Who does the Mental Capacity Act apply to?

The MCA applies to all people working with and caring for those for whom they make decisions for or are acting in connection with those who may lack capacity to make particular decisions.

The MCA imposes a duty on health professionals and other healthcare staff to have regard to the Code of Practice. Those who are legally required to have regard to the Code of Practice when acting in relation to a person who lacks, or who may lack, capacity are as follows:

People working in a professional capacity may include:
➤ doctors
➤ nurses
➤ social workers
➤ dentists
➤ psychologists
➤ psychotherapists.

People who are being paid to provide care or support may include:
➤ care assistants
➤ home care workers
➤ support workers
➤ staff working in supported housing
➤ prison officers
➤ paramedics
➤ anyone who is a deputy appointed by the Court of Protection
➤ anyone acting as an IMCA
➤ anyone carrying out research involving people who cannot make a decision about taking part.

Criminal offence
Under the MCA it is a criminal offence to ill-treat or wilfully neglect someone who lacks capacity by someone with responsibility for their care or with decision-making powers.

General principles under the MCA
No one can consent to the examination or treatment of an adult who lacks capacity to give consent for themselves, unless they have been authorised to do so under a Lasting Power of Attorney or they have the authority to make treatment decisions as a court appointed deputy. Therefore, in most cases, parents, relatives or members of the healthcare team cannot consent on behalf of such an adult. However, there are exceptions to this. The MCA sets out circumstances in which it will be lawful to carry out such examinations or treatment without consent.

Generally, the refusal of treatment made by a person when they had capacity cannot be overridden if the advance decision is valid and applicable to the situation. There are certain statutory exceptions to this principle, including treatment for mental disorder under the Mental Health Act 1983.[6]

The exemptions are discussed in more detail below.

Five core principles

There are five key principles that underpin the MCA.[7] These principles must be followed in any assessment of or decision about a person's capacity.

The five core principles are:

1 A person must be assumed to have capacity unless it is established that they lack capacity.
2 A person is not to be treated as unable to make a decision unless all practicable (doable) steps to help them to do so have been taken without success.
3 A person is not to be treated as unable to make a decision merely because they make an unwise decision.
4 An act done, or decision made, under the MCA for or on behalf of a person who lacks capacity must be done, or made, in their best interests.
5 Before the act is done, or the decision is made, regard must be had to whether the purpose for which it is needed can be as effectively achieved in a way that is less restrictive of the person's rights and freedom of action.

The two-stage test

In order to decide whether an individual has the capacity to make a particular decision the health professional must answer two questions:

> Stage 1: Is there an impairment, or disturbance in the functioning of, a person's mind or brain? If so,
>
> Stage 2: Is the impairment or disturbance sufficient that the person lacks the capacity to make a particular decision?

The MCA says that a person is unable to make their own decision if they cannot do one or more of the following four things:

1 understand information given to them
2 retain that information long enough to be able to make the decision
3 weigh up the information available to make the decision
4 communicate their decision – this could be by talking, using sign language or even simple muscle movements such as blinking an eye or squeezing a hand.

Every effort should be made to find ways of communicating with someone before deciding that they lack capacity to make a decision based solely on their inability to communicate. The health professional will need to involve family, friends, carers or other professionals. These issues are explained further below.

WHAT IS MENTAL CAPACITY?

Mental capacity within the context of the MCA means the ability to make a decision.[8]

A person lacks capacity if they are unable to make a particular decision because of an impairment or disturbance of the mind or brain, whether temporary or permanent, at the time the decision needs to be made.

The starting point is always that most people will be able to make most decisions most of the time. There should be a presumption that an adult has capacity to consent to treatment unless you can show otherwise.

A health professional cannot decide that someone lacks capacity just by a person's age, appearance, condition or an aspect of their behaviour that might lead to unjustified assumptions about capacity. The fact that someone has dementia or a learning disability does not mean that they lack capacity. No such assumption of capacity must ever be made. A reason to impose treatment when someone refuses treatment which may result in their death is an unnatural reaction and this must never be made.

EXAMPLE 1

Lucy has severe learning disabilities and lives in a care home. She is able to choose what to eat and drink and makes these decisions for herself. She does not always have the capacity to decide on appropriate clothing for the weather, and care assistants make these decisions for her when necessary.

EXAMPLE 2

Joan has suffered a stroke. Her speech is slurred and she sounds incoherent. She enters into a new tenancy agreement with the advice of her support worker, and signs the paperwork with a cross, as she is no longer able to write her name after her stroke. Joan has the capacity to make this decision, and staff should not assume otherwise.

You cannot decide that someone lacks capacity based on a person's age, appearance, condition or an aspect of their behaviour that might lead to unjustified assumptions about capacity. In Example 2, although the housing officer may not be sure whether Joan is able to understand what she is signing as her speech sounded slurred and incoherent, her support worker is able to assure the housing officer that Joan understood sufficiently and that his assumptions were not justified.

CAPACITY IS TIME AND DECISION SPECIFIC

Capacity is both time and decision specific. Most people will be able to make most decisions most of the time.

A lack of capacity can change over time; a person may have the capacity to make some decisions but not others.

TEMPORARY, FLUCTUATING AND LONG-STANDING CAPACITY

Capacity may vary. It may be temporary, may fluctuate or may be long-standing.

A person's capacity to make a decision can be affected by a range of factors such as:
- stroke
- dementia
- learning disability
- mental illness.

Physical conditions can also affect capacity, such as:
- intimidating or unfamiliar environment
- trauma
- shock
- loss
- health problems.

Temporary incapacity

A patient may lack capacity temporarily. A patient's capacity to understand may be temporarily affected by factors such as being unconscious due to an accident, shock, panic, fatigue, pain, medication, being under anaesthetic or under sedation in intensive care for a period of days or weeks or under the influence of alcohol or drugs.

Where possible, the procedure should be delayed and the health professional should wait until they regain capacity and then obtain their consent for any additional procedure. If it is known that the patient is likely to be incapacitated, for example following a procedure it is necessary for them to be in intensive care for a period of time, then any likely or additional procedures should be explored with the patient before carrying out the operation so as to pre-empt any difficulties with consent.

Any intervention is only permitted to be made which is necessary and no more than is reasonably required in the patient's best interests pending the recovery of capacity. This will include, but is not limited to, routine procedures such as washing and assistance with feeding. If a medical intervention is thought to be in the patient's best interests but can be delayed until the patient recovers capacity and can consent to, or refuse, the intervention, it must be delayed until that time.

EXAMPLE

John is having cardiac surgery. Following the procedure he will be in intensive care for a week. Following surgery he suffers complications and requires further surgery. John has not given consent for any other procedures.

If the additional surgery is in John's best interest but can wait until he regains consciousness, then surgery should be delayed. Once John regains capacity then his consent may be sought (or refused) for the additional procedure.

Only if the surgery is necessary in an emergency in order to save John's life can it proceed, but this is not the best way to manage this situation. Advising John of the known risks of the procedure would have been discussed as part of the consent process for the original surgery. It would have also been prudent to obtain information about John's wishes in the event of the risks manifesting and to have obtained consent for any additional procedures that may become necessary.

Fluctuating capacity

Capacity may fluctuate. This may include a patient who, due to pain, treatment or condition, may, for example, have good days and bad days. Some days they have capacity and some days they may not. In these circumstances, it is good practice to establish, while the person has capacity, their views about any treatment that may be necessary during a period of incapacity.

The health professional must clearly document the patient's views.

EXAMPLE

Esther has had a stroke. She is able to make decisions about most things most days. Occasionally she has a bad day and is very confused and sleepy.

The health professional should wait a day or so until Esther has a good day and when she has capacity they should then obtain consent from Esther to treatment.

Where a patient's condition is likely to continue to deteriorate over time, such as an inoperable brain tumour effecting cognitive function, the health professional should consider what other matters and views should be explored while they have capacity and obtain their views.

People with a mental illness do not necessarily lack capacity. However, people with a severe mental illness may experience a temporary loss or fluctuating loss of capacity to make decisions about their care and treatment.

Long-standing capacity

Capacity may be long standing, such as someone who has brain damage from birth or someone who has suffered brain damage due to an accident or illness.

Health professionals should not assume that the patient does not have capacity and should make every effort to communicate with the patient. Where the patient has never been competent, it may be difficult to determine what is in the patient's best interests by reference to earlier, competent, beliefs and values. In such cases, family and friends close to the patient will often be in the best position to advise health professionals on the patient's needs and preferences, likes and dislikes so that the health professional can determine what is in the patient's best interest.

It must also be noted that a person may have capacity to make decisions about some things but not others. The greater the complexity of the issue to be decided, the greater the capacity they will need.

ASSESSING CAPACITY

What triggers an assessment?

Health professionals should always start from the presumption that the patient has capacity. Doubts as to a person's capacity to make a particular decision can occur because of:

➤ the way a person behaves
➤ their circumstances
➤ concerns raised by someone else.

EXAMPLE

John has moderate learning disabilities and autism. He makes most decisions about his finances, but he has a new girlfriend and is now spending considerable amounts of money on new clothes. He has stopped contributing money to the household budget of the group home where he lives. His care manager decides to call a meeting with others involved in his support to discuss the managers concerns.

In this example, the trigger is John's behaviour.

Remember that an unwise decision does not necessarily indicate lack of capacity.

EXAMPLE

David suffers from diabetes. He is refusing to take his medication and as a result his condition is deteriorating. He has developed sores and he does not want them to be treated or dressed.

The fact that David is refusing treatment does mean he lacks capacity, even where his condition may deteriorate.

Health professionals should inform David of the treatment options and risks as well as information of having no treatment at all. Health professionals should work in partnership with David but they must respect his wishes.

> **EXAMPLE**
>
> Mary suffered a stroke some years ago. She has little or no use in her arm. Her speech is slurred. She is cared for at home. Yesterday she suffered a minor fall. Since then Mary cannot now recall her name or her address. She cannot recall if she has any family. She no longer recognises her carer. She has no recollection of the fall. She is drifting in and out of sleep. The carer calls the GP.

Does Mary's behaviour give rise to the question of capacity?

The fact that Mary suffered a stroke and has slurred speech does not render her lacking capacity. However, the fact that she no longer recognises her carer may trigger the issue of capacity and invoke an assessment.

MAKING AN ASSESSMENT

The starting point is that a person has capacity to make the decision in question. A finding that a person lacks capacity to make a decision should not be made lightly.

A formal, clear and recorded process should be followed when an important decision such as a move or medical decision is to be made.

There is a two-stage test that must be used when assessing capacity:[9]

1   Is the patient suffering from an impairment of or disturbance in the functioning of the mind or brain?
2   Is the effect of the impairment or disturbance an inability to make a decision?

This two-stage test must be used, and health professionals must be able to show it has been used. Remember that an unwise decision made by the person does not of itself indicate a lack of capacity.

Most people will be able to make most decisions, even when they have a label or diagnosis that may seem to imply that they cannot. This is a general principle that cannot be over-emphasised.

The assessment process has to be clear and accountable. It will require input from health professionals and other staff in the range of organisations involved in providing support, and should include family and carers.

Under the MCA, the following factors have to be considered when assessing if someone has capacity to make a decision. Any assessment of a person's

capacity must consider the following factors:
- ➤ whether they are able to understand the information
- ➤ whether they are able to retain the information related to the decision to be made
- ➤ whether they are able to use or weigh that information as part of the process of making the decision.

The person has to be able to do all three to make a decision and they have to be able to communicate that decision.

Health professionals must also consider whether they are able to communicate that decision. This may be by any means, non-verbal communication including sign language, blinking an eye or squeezing a hand.

Often family members are able to assist in providing information on how best the patient may communicate.

Communication cannot be over-emphasised. Health professionals would have seen patients who, despite having significant brain damage, can communicate even where their only form of communication is to scream. The parents and family will know if they are tired, hot, cold, happy, in pain and so on. Health professionals must make every effort to communicate and not just assume that they lack capacity to make all decisions.

Communication passport

Health professionals may like to use a communication passport for communication and consultations. This is a useful tool.

EXAMPLE

Susan, whose daughter Emily has multiple disabilities and no speech, has made a communication passport that can be used to help staff communicate with Emily in relation to the decisions she can make.

The 'communication passport' explains what the emotional responses mean, as far as they are able to do so. Each day, wherever the patient is, health professionals record what the patient has done and what the responses to certain activities are. This gives health professionals a long-term view on what the patient is trying to tell them about the services and assists health professionals in voicing the decisions that the patient makes through non-verbal communication. The communication passport should be placed with the records and all health professionals caring for the patient should read it.

Where there is no family or carer or other person authorised to make decisions for that person, an independent mental capacity advocate (IMCA) may be assigned if there is an important decision about certain medical treatment or a change of accommodation to be made. Other advocates may also be able to offer support, representation or advice, and staff need to be familiar with the local services and know how to contact them. The role and responsibilities of the IMCA is explained in detail post.

All health professionals and staff involved in an assessment should keep good accurate records that explain the grounds on which a person is found to have, or lack, capacity.

Day-to-day assessments of capacity may be relatively informal but still should be written in the records. This may require a shift in practice, as many of these informal decisions have been made in the past without being recognised as decisions about capacity. For example, a home care worker may have undertaken food shopping for an older person with dementia without consulting them about what they would like to eat. If there are no ways of seeking their views on this and they are not able to contribute to decisions about what food should be bought, this should be discussed with the home care worker's supervisor and the decisions recorded.

Blanket decisions

Assessing capacity is personal to the individual patient concerned.

> I know of a place where staff working in a group home for people with learning disabilities have always looked after the residents' money for them.

The MCA has the effect that 'blanket decisions' like this about groups of service users cannot be made. Health professionals will have to assess the capacity of individual residents to make particular decisions for themselves and record these decisions.

Making the assessment

Those being assessed for capacity to make a decision should be assessed at their best level of functioning for the decision to be taken.

Who should assess capacity?

Generally, the health professional treating or caring for the patient can assess the patients' capacity or could be involved in making an assessment. If the health professional has any concerns over capacity they may wish to seek peer review or advice from another health professional such as the GP or a doctor. It is not necessary to always consult a psychiatrist on matters of capacity although there may be circumstances where it is appropriate to seek such advice. This is discussed further below.

Remember, each decision needs to be considered alongside the person's capacity to make it. For example, care home staff may regularly make day-to-day assessments of capacity when asking residents whether they want to do one thing or another. One person may be able to choose whether to use an incontinence pad, while others lack the capacity to make this decision.

The more significant the decision to be made, the more likely that a number of different professional staff will be involved.

For example, doctors, nursing staff, social care staff and his relative will all contribute to the assessment of his capacity to make the decision about moving.

EXAMPLE

Phillip lives in a care home but his dementia is causing him great distress. Fellow residents are also upset by his actions, even though they know he is ill. Does he have capacity to consent to move to a new home where staff may be able to offer him more support? This is a decision where the views of several professionals, including his GP, the consultant psychogeriatrician, the community nurse who sees him regularly and the home manager, will be required. The care manager is responsible for coordinating the assessment of Phillip's capacity to make this decision. The care manager will also find it helpful to talk to Denise, Phillip's great-niece, who has known him for many years and still visits him occasionally.

Assessing capacity will always depend upon the individual being assessed. Medical assessment, for example, while relevant, would not necessarily be the only, or even the main, assessment method. Specialist or expert opinion may be helpful sometimes, but knowledge of the person concerned, for example that of family and friends, is very important. Remember though, as noted above, most people are able to make most decisions.

What sort of help might a person need to make a decision?

You must always bear in mind the five core principles and ensure that no one is treated as unable to make a decision unless all practicable steps to help them have been exhausted and shown not to work.

The following factors demonstrate the range of areas that will need to be considered. The range of areas to be considered will be specific to the individual and their circumstances, and the two-stage test of capacity, stated earlier, must be applied.

Steps to be taken

The Code of Practice sets out the steps to be taken.[10]

➤ Provide all relevant information but do not burden the person with more detail than required. Include information on the consequences of making, or not making, the decision. Provide similar information on any alternative options.

➤ Consult with family and other people who know the person well on the best way to communicate, e.g. by using pictures or signing. Check if there is someone who is good at communicating with the person involved.

➤ Be aware of any cultural, ethnic or religious factors which may have a bearing on the individual. Consider whether an advocate or someone else could assist, e.g. a member of a religious or community group to which the person belongs.

➤ Make the person feel at ease by selecting an environment that suits them. Make sure it is quiet and unlikely to be interrupted. Arrange to visit relevant locations; for example, if the decision is about a hospital or short-break stay, visit the place with them. See if a relative or friend can be with them to support them.

➤ Try to choose the best time for the person. Try to ensure that the effects of any medication or treatment are considered. For example, if any medication makes a person drowsy, see them before they take the medication, or after the effect has worn off.

➤ Take time. Make one decision at a time, don't rush and be prepared to try more than once.

Factors to be considered in an assessment:
- general intellectual ability
- memory
- attention and concentration
- reasoning
- information processing – how a person interprets what they are told
- verbal comprehension and all forms of communication
- cultural influences
- social context
- ability to communicate.

Not all of these factors need to be considered in every assessment of capacity although, for some formal assessments, a number of these factors will be relevant.

A reasonable belief in a person's lack of capacity to make a particular decision should be supported by judgments about some of these factors.

Each assessment of capacity will vary according to the type of decision and the individual circumstances. The more complex or serious the decision, the greater the level of capacity required. The following questions in line with the Code of Practice must be addressed:

Questions to consider[11]
- Does the person have a general understanding of what decision they need to make and why they need to make it?
- Do they understand the consequences of making, or not making, the decision, or of deciding one way or another?
- Are they able to understand the information relevant to the decision?
- Can they weigh up the relative importance of the information?
- Can they use and retain the information as part of the decision-making process?

BEST INTERESTS

Acting in a person's best interests

The Mental Capacity Act (MCA) requires any decision or act made on behalf of a person who lacks capacity to be made in that person's best interests. Decisions may be made under the MCA by people appointed to do so, such as attorneys, deputies and the Court of Protection. As stated previously, decisions will often be made by health professionals and those involved in the care and treatment of the person concerned. Health professionals can also undertake most acts in connection with care or treatment which are made on behalf of a person who lacks capacity to consent if those acts are in a person's best interests.[12]

The MCA does not define best interests but identifies a range of factors that must be considered when determining the best interests of individuals who have been assessed as lacking capacity to make a particular decision or consent to acts of care or treatment. There are a number of steps involved in deciding what a person's best interests are. The MCA makes it clear that when determining what is in someone's best interests, you must not base the decision on the person's age or appearance or make unjustified assumptions based on their condition.

The factors that must be taken into account when determining what is in someone's best interests are set out in the best interests checklist.[13]

Best interests checklist

Considering all relevant circumstances	These are circumstances of which the decision-maker is aware and those which it is reasonable to regard as relevant.
Regaining capacity	Can the decision be put off until the person regains capacity?
Permitting and encouraging participation	This may involve finding the appropriate means of communication or using other people to help the person participate in the decision-making process.
Special considerations for life-sustaining treatment	The person making the best-interests decision must not be motivated by the desire to bring about a person's death.
Considering the person's wishes, feelings, beliefs and values	Especially any written statements made by the person when they had capacity.
Taking into account the views of other people	Take account of the views of family and informal carers and anyone with an interest in the person's welfare or appointed to act on the person's behalf.
	Taking into account the views of any independent mental capacity advocate (IMCA) or any attorney appointed by the person or deputy appointed by the Court of Protection.
Consider whether there is a less restrictive alternative	Consider whether there is a less restrictive alternative or intervention that is in the person's best interests.
Other good practice points include	Demonstrating that you have carefully assessed any conflicting evidence. Providing clear, objective reasons as to why you are acting in the person's best interests.

> ### EXAMPLE
>
> Joanne, who has severe brain damage, is looked after at home by her parents and attends a day centre for two days a week. The day centre workers are taking some of the service users horse riding at the local stables. Joanne's parents want her to be included in activities at the centre but are anxious that she won't be able to manage a horse. Joanne seems excited at the idea of going to the stables.
>
> Her parents and staff discuss the situation and decide to ask a care assistant who has a good relationship with Joanne and who can understand her communication to accompany her to the riding stables and keep an eye on her.

Acting in a person's best interests can involve negotiating a compromise between different views and wishes.

ACTS IN CONNECTION WITH CARE AND TREATMENT

Personal care

Acts in connection with personal care may include:

➤ assistance with physical care, e.g. washing, dressing, toileting, changing a catheter and colostomy care
➤ help with eating and drinking
➤ help with travelling
➤ shopping
➤ paying bills
➤ household maintenance
➤ those relating to community care services.

Healthcare and treatment

Acts connected to healthcare and treatment may include:

➤ administering medication
➤ diabetes injections
➤ diagnostic examinations and tests
➤ medical and dental treatment
➤ nursing care
➤ emergency procedures.

Health professionals must also consider whether they could provide the care or treatment in a less restrictive way, for example, could a person be given a shower that they can manage themselves rather than a bath for which they will need to be supervised?

Who is the 'decision-maker'?

The 'decision-maker' is a term for someone who has to decide whether to provide care or treatment for someone who cannot consent because they lack the capacity to do so.

The decision-maker will vary depending on the individual's circumstances and the type of decision involved. Social care staff will be decision-makers for many day-to-day situations.

They may also act as decision-makers for longer-term decisions regarding the care of an individual who lacks capacity. Those making such decisions have some protection under the MCA.[14]

Health professionals will be decision-makers for medical and related treatment, such as dental care and physiotherapy.

'Treatment' includes investigations such as X-rays, as well as procedures like operations and injections.

However, doctors are unlikely to be decision-makers for social activities or day-to-day care. Nurses will be the decision-makers in relation to nursing care.

Remember, the person delivering the treatment or nursing care makes the decision about whether to deliver the care, even though the treatment may have been prescribed by someone else.

Although decisions may result from discussions with other professionals or with the medical or nursing team, the person who delivers the treatment or care for somebody who lacks capacity is responsible for making the final decision to deliver that treatment or care in the person's best interests.

Family members and unpaid carers who live with or care for people who lack capacity to make decisions will often be the decision-makers for many day-to-day acts such as what people eat or wear.

DEPRIVATION OF LIBERTY

The Bournewood case[15]

The Bournewood case is a legal case that tested the boundary between appropriate restraint or restriction and the loss of human rights under Article 5 of the European Convention on Human Rights (ECHR)[16] – the right to liberty. The MCA was amended to take into account the issues raised by this case.

CASE

The patient was in hospital and lacked the capacity to say whether he would stay in hospital and accept treatment. He was not detained under the Mental Health Act 1983.

In this case a 49-year-old severely autistic man, known as HL, who could not speak, was admitted to Bournewood psychiatric hospital, Surrey, after becoming distressed at a day centre.

When the day centre staff were unable to contact HL's carers and could not contain the situation, a GP tried to calm him down with medication. This was unsuccessful so the GP referred him to the local hospital where he was seen by a psychiatrist. The psychiatrist couldn't tell whether HL had a psychiatric condition or behavioural problem, so decided to admit him for observation. When he was discharged just over four months later, his carers claimed HL looked like 'someone out of Belsen'.

HL's carers made an application to the court to determine if informal admission to hospital was unlawful, even though he was incapable of agreeing to or refusing treatment. The case went through several court processes at the Court of Appeal, the High Court and the European Court of Human Rights.

The European Court of Human Rights determined that the healthcare professionals treating and managing HL exercised complete and effective control over his care and movements. He was under continuous supervision and control and was not free to leave. The court ruled that HL had been deprived of his right to liberty under Article 5 of the Human Rights Convention. HL had not been detained under the Mental Health Act 1983, instead he was accommodated in his own 'best interests' under the common law doctrine of 'necessity'. The European Court held that this doctrine was too arbitrary and lacked the safeguards provided to those sectioned under the Mental Health Act.

The distinction between restraint and the loss of liberty, which took this case to the European Court, is 'one of degree and intensity, not one of nature and substance'. Any deprivation of liberty can only be lawful if accompanied by safeguards similar to those surrounding detention under the Mental Health Act 1983.

Closing the 'Bournewood gap'

The numbers of non-compliant patients being held against their will is unknown, but in a consultation between March and June 2005 to seek views on potential ways to close the 'Bournewood gap', the government estimated it could be as many as 50000 of those permanently admitted to care homes and 22000 hospital in-patients.

The consultation resulted in the introduction of safeguards for people who lack capacity and are detained for treatment or care. The deprivation of liberty safeguards, which came into force in April 2009, provides a framework for authorising and challenging detentions.

The Mental Health Act 2007[17] – as well as amending the Mental Health Act 1983 – was used as the vehicle for introducing deprivation of liberty safeguards into the Mental Capacity Act 2005. The safeguards strengthen the rights of hospital patients and those in care homes, as well as ensuring compliance with the European Convention on Human Rights.

The safeguards include:

➤ A third party, such as a relative or carer, can request an assessment of whether or not a person is being deprived of their liberty.
➤ Anyone who does not have family or friends who can be consulted will have an independent mental capacity advocate instructed to support and represent them during the assessment process. IMCAs will also be a right for those whose representative or supervisory authority believes it is necessary.

MCA and deprivation of liberty

In circumstances where restraint needs to be used, staff restraining a person who lacks capacity will be protected from liability, for example criminal charges, if certain conditions are met.

There are specific rules on the use of restraint, whether verbal or physical, and the restriction or deprivation of liberty. This is outlined in the Code of Practice, 6.11–6.19 and 6.40–6.53.[18]

If restraint is used, health professionals must reasonably believe that the person lacks capacity to consent to the act in question, that it needs to be done in their best interests and that restraint is necessary to protect the person from harm. It must also be a proportionate or a reasonable response to the likelihood of the person suffering harm and the seriousness of that harm. Restraint can include physical restraint, restricting the person's freedom of movement and verbal warnings, but cannot extend to depriving someone of their liberty.

Restraint may also be used under common law in circumstances where there is a risk that the person lacking capacity may harm someone else.

Questions to be asked in determining if authorisation for deprivation of liberty is required:

➤ Does the patient lack capacity?
➤ Is the patient at risk of deprivation of liberty within 28 days?
➤ Can the patient receive care through a less restrictive but still effective alternative?
➤ Is the person 18 years of age or older (or going to turn 18 years within 28 days)?
➤ Is the person subject to the powers of the MHA which would mean they are ineligible for deprivation of liberty?
➤ Has the person made an advance decision to refuse the treatment?
➤ Is the proposed deprivation of liberty for mental health treatment in hospital and does the patient object?
➤ Has the person's attorney/deputy indicated they will refuse on their behalf?
➤ Should deprivation of liberty begin immediately?

The answers to these questions will determine if authorisation is required.

Checklist for authorisation

Questions	If the answer is NO	If the answer is YES
Does the patient lack capacity?	No application can be made	Application may be required
Is the patient at risk of deprivation of liberty within 28 days?	Reconsider when reviewing care	Application may be required
Can the patient receive care through less restrictive but still effective alternative?	Application may be required	Application cannot be made
Is the person 18 years of age or older (or going to turn 18 years within 28 days)?	No application can be made – consider Children Act or MHA	Application may be required

Questions	If the answer is NO	If the answer is YES
Is the person subject to the powers of the MHA which would mean they are ineligible for deprivation of liberty?	Application may be required	Application cannot be made
Has the person made an advance decision to refuse the treatment?	Application may be required	Application cannot be made
Is the proposed deprivation of liberty for mental health treatment in hospital and does the patient object?	Application may be required	Application cannot be made
Has the person's attorney/deputy indicated they will refuse on their behalf?	Application is required	Application cannot be made
Should deprivation of liberty begin immediately?	Apply for standard authorisation	Grant Urgent Authorisation

---

EXAMPLE

Mandy, who has severe learning disabilities, likes to visit the nearby park but often wants to climb over the fence around the pond. Staff from the centre she attends generally avoid this by distracting her, but on occasion they do have to stop her climbing over the fence. They have shared their ideas about which distractions work best, but sometimes it is necessary to stop Mandy from potentially injuring herself or getting very distressed. They have a plan for restraining her in this situation which is recorded in her care plan.

If Mandy had an appointed attorney or deputy, staff might have to seek their permission for this plan.

Section 5 of the MCA,[19] which provides protection from liability in certain circumstances, will not protect health professionals from liability for any action they take that conflicts with a decision made by someone acting under a Lasting Power of Attorney or a deputy appointed by the Court of Protection, whose authority extends to such decisions, nor does it protect staff against negligent acts.

LASTING POWERS OF ATTORNEY

What is a Lasting Power of Attorney?

A Lasting Power of Attorney (LPA) is a legal document to appoint someone to handle the financial or welfare affairs, during lifetime of a person.

The LPA replaced the Enduring Power of Attorney (EPA).[20] Under a LPA[21] an individual can, while they still have capacity, appoint another person to make decisions on their behalf about financial, welfare or health-care matters. The person making the LPA chooses who will be their attorney. They can give power to the attorney to make all decisions or they can choose which decisions they can make.

An LPA can be created at any time. This does not mean that the donor immediately foregoes the right to carry on dealing with their own affairs. They can go on doing this for as long as they are able or wish to do so. The important thing is that the LPA is ready to use in the future, should the donor become mentally incapable or feel they can no longer cope with managing things themselves. It would be prudent to register the LPA immediately (at the Office of the Public Guardian) so it can be used in an emergency. A mentally capable donor can cancel an LPA at any time.

When acting under an LPA, an attorney has authority to make decisions on behalf of the person who made it if they can no longer make these decisions for themselves. In these cases, an attorney is not there simply to be consulted, although they should still be consulted if appropriate where other decisions are being made. Attorneys must act in accordance with the Code of Practice.

There are two different forms of LPA

People can choose one or both. These are:
1 personal welfare, including healthcare
2 property and affairs (financial matters).

The person making the LPA is the donor, who donates or hands over responsibility to make decisions under specified circumstances.

The person appointed to make the decisions under the LPA is the donee, also known as the attorney. One attorney may hold a number of LPAs for different people; for example, a daughter can have LPAs for both her parents. A bank official can have LPAs for a number of clients. A person can choose one or a number of people to hold their LPA, such as a partner and adult children.

If a personal welfare LPA is in place but does not include the authority to make the decisions which now need to be made, health and social care professionals will make the necessary best interests decisions, but they should consult with the attorney.

When is an LPA valid?[22]

In order to be valid, an LPA must be set out on the right form and registered with the Office of the Public Guardian before it can be used. An LPA is a formal, legal document. A personal welfare LPA will only take effect when a person has lost capacity to make a particular decision. If it is not registered with the Office of the Public Guardian, it cannot be used. An LPA concerning financial matters will take effect immediately it is registered, unless the donor specifies that it should not take effect until they lose capacity to make these decisions.

Who can be an attorney?

It is up to the donor to choose whom they wish to appoint as their attorney. An attorney could be a family member or a friend, or a professional such as a lawyer.

The Code of Practice advises that health and social care professionals should not act as attorneys for people they are supporting unless they are also close relatives of the person who lacks capacity.

EXAMPLE

Mrs Rees has never trusted doctors and prefers to rely on alternative therapies. She saw her father suffer after invasive treatment for cancer. She is clear that she would refuse such treatment even if she might die without it.

Mrs Rees is diagnosed with cancer and discusses her wishes with her husband. She trusts her husband to respect her wishes about the form of treatment she would, or would not, accept. She asks him to act as her attorney to make health and welfare decisions on her behalf should she lack the capacity in the future.

Mrs Rees makes a personal welfare LPA, appointing her husband to make all her welfare decisions, including the authorisation to refuse life-sustaining treatment, on her behalf.

If his wife loses capacity to make her own decisions, Mr Rees will be able to make decisions about treatment in her best interests, once the LPA is registered, taking into account what he knows about her feelings.

Attorneys, like everyone else, are always subject to the provisions of the Mental Capacity Act (MCA), particularly the core principles and the best interests requirements. An attorney must be over 18 years old and must not be bankrupt (for property and affairs LPAs only). Most attorneys will be named individuals. However, for property and affairs LPAs, the attorney could be a trust or part of a bank.

Powers of and limitations on LPAs

An LPA can be used to set out a person's wishes and preferences, which an attorney must then take into account when determining the person's best interests. For example, a person may want their attorney to take their religious beliefs into account when making decisions for them in the future.

However, it is important to remember that an attorney can consent to or refuse treatment as specified by the donor in the LPA, but an attorney has no power to demand a specific treatment that healthcare professionals do not believe is clinically necessary or appropriate.

If the donor has not specified any limits to the attorney's authority, the attorney will be able to make all decisions on their behalf. However, they will only be able to refuse life-sustaining treatment if this has been specified in the LPA.

An attorney acting under a property and affairs LPA can only make certain gifts from the property and estate of the donor, for example to friends and relatives, including the attorney themselves, and on customary occasions such as birthdays, Christmas, Divali or any other religious festival the person lacking capacity would be likely to celebrate. Any customary gift or charitable donation must be reasonable in the circumstances. Limitations may also be specified in the LPA. The Court of Protection can give an attorney permission to make additional gifts if the attorney seeks the Court's approval.

Enduring Powers of Attorney

Enduring Powers of Attorney (EPAs)[23] were established by the Enduring Powers of Attorney Act 1985. They allow the appointed attorney to manage property and financial affairs on behalf of the donor. At the onset of the donor's incapacity, the attorney must register the EPA with the Office of the Public Guardian in order for their authorisation under the EPA to continue. No new EPAs can be set up but existing EPAs will continue to be valid whether registered or not (Code of Practice, chapter 7). Donors can choose to replace their existing EPA with an LPA if they still have capacity.

LPA forms

There have been recent changes to the Lasting Power of Attorney (LPA) forms which came into use on 1 October 2009. The existing forms were too long, too complicated and solicitor's fees to help complete them were very expensive. Too many forms were being returned because of errors. The new forms are easier to complete.

RESOLVING DISPUTES

Health professionals may come across a situation where there is a dispute between family and health professionals or between family members. For example, there may be a dispute about what is in the patient's best interests.

The Code of Practice[24] is clear that any dispute about the best interests of a person who lacks capacity should be resolved, wherever possible, in a quick and cost-effective manner. Alternative solutions to disputes should be considered, where appropriate, before any application to the Court of Protection. The Court will consider if appropriate alternatives have been pursued when an application is made. Certain groups, including people who lack or are said to lack capacity to make a decision, have an automatic right of application to the Court. Otherwise, the Court will decide which applications it will accept.

Alternative methods for resolving disputes include the following:

➤ Disputes or arguments between family members may be dealt within formally or through mediation.
➤ Disputes about health, social or other welfare services may be dealt with by informal or formal complaints processes such as Patient Advice and Liaison Services (PALS) in the NHS in England or through other existing complaints systems.
➤ Advocacy services may be able to help resolve a dispute.

Disputes regarding certain medical treatments may go directly to the Court of Protection.

THE COURT OF PROTECTION AND DEPUTIES[25]

What is the Court of Protection?

The Court of Protection is a specialist court with powers to deal with matters affecting adults who may lack capacity to make particular decisions. The Court is able to hear cases at a number of locations in England and Wales. It covers all areas of decision-making under the Mental Capacity Act (MCA) and can determine whether a person has capacity in relation to a particular decision, whether a proposed action would be lawful, whether a particular act or decision is in a person's best interests and the meaning or effect of a Lasting Power of Attorney (LPA) in disputed cases.

The Court of Protection plans to be an accessible, regional court. It aims to be informal and quick. It takes over the duties of the former Court of Protection and matters regarding healthcare and personal welfare that were previously dealt with by the High Court. It is expected that the Court of Protection will only be involved where particularly complex decisions or difficult disputes are involved.

Either the Court of Protection or the Family Court may deal with health and welfare decisions concerning 16 and 17-year-olds who lack capacity to make particular decisions.

EXAMPLE

Mark has been diagnosed with a rare disease. His prognosis is poor. His family and healthcare providers have become aware of a new treatment which is reported to produce improvements in some patients but it has side-effects.

Mark lacks capacity to consent to the treatment. The consultant, who is the decision-maker regarding Michael's treatment, wants to use this treatment but Mark's family are unhappy about the side-effects and believe that treatment would not be in Mark's best interests. Because of the difference in opinion, an application is made to the Court of Protection for a declaration that it would be lawful, and in Mark's best interests, to receive the treatment.

The Court, after considering evidence from all relevant parties, makes such a declaration and Mark receives the treatment.

What is a court-appointed deputy?[26]

The MCA requires the Court to make a decision where possible. However, the Court might decide that it is appropriate to appoint a deputy. Deputies are appointed by the Court of Protection to make ongoing decisions on behalf of a person who lacks capacity to make those decisions.

A deputy can be appointed to deal with financial matters and or personal welfare. The appointment of a deputy could take place, for example, where no Lasting Power of Attorney exists or there is a serious dispute among carers that cannot be resolved in any other way. The appointment of a deputy is limited in scope – what it can do and duration – time. This is to reflect the principle of the less restrictive intervention.

A deputy can be a family member, or any other person (or in property and affairs cases, a trust) the Court thinks suitable. A deputy must act with regard to the Code of Practice, in accordance with the Act's principles and in the person's best interests.

THE MENTAL CAPACITY ACT 2005 AND ADVANCE DECISIONS TO REFUSE TREATMENT

This is discussed in detail in Chapter 18.[27,28]

INDEPENDENT MENTAL CAPACITY ADVOCATES (IMCAS)[29]

Sometimes a patient does not have any family or friends that can advocate for them if they lose capacity. This can leave the patient vulnerable.

The Mental Capacity Act (MCA) and Mental Health Act 2007[30] introduces a duty on the NHS and local authorities to involve an independent mental capacity advocate (IMCA) in certain decisions. This ensures that, when a person who lacks capacity to make a decision has no one who can speak for them and serious medical treatment or a move into accommodation arranged by the local authority or NHS body (following an assessment under the NHS and Community Care Act 1990)[31] is being considered, an IMCA is instructed.

The IMCA has a specific role to play in supporting and representing a person who lacks capacity to make the decision in question. They are only able to act for people whose care or treatment is arranged by a local authority or the NHS. They have the right to information about an individual, so they can see relevant health and social care records.

The duties of an IMCA are to:

➤ support the person who lacks capacity and represent their views and interests to the decision-maker

➤ obtain and evaluate information, both through interviewing the person and through examining relevant records and documents

➤ obtain the views of professionals and paid workers providing care or treatment for the person who lacks capacity

➤ identify alternative courses of action

➤ obtain a further medical opinion, if required

➤ prepare a report (that the decision-maker must consider).

In England, regulations have extended the role of IMCAs so they may also be asked to represent the person lacking capacity where there is an allegation of or evidence of abuse or neglect to or by a person who lacks capacity. In adult protection cases, an IMCA can be appointed even though the person has family or friends.

Similarly, the regulations also allow IMCAs to contribute to reviews for people who have been in accommodation arranged by the local authority or NHS body or who have been in hospital for more than 12 weeks and who have nobody else to represent them.

The local authority or NHS body may instruct an IMCA to represent the person lacking capacity in either adult protection cases or accommodation reviews if they consider that it would be of 'particular benefit' to the person. The National Assembly for Wales has also extended the role of IMCAs in Wales, to cover accommodation reviews and adult protection cases.

IMCAs always represent the interests of those who have been assessed as lacking capacity to make a major decision about serious medical treatment or a longer-term accommodation move, if they have no one else to speak for them other than paid carers, and if their care or accommodation is arranged by their local authority or NHS.

IMCAs may represent the interests of those who have been placed in accommodation by the NHS or local authority, and whose accommodation arrangements are being reviewed, and/or those who have been or are alleged to have been abused or neglected or where a person lacking capacity has been alleged or proven to be an abuser (even if they have friends or family).

An IMCA is not a decision-maker for the person who lacks capacity. They are there to support and represent that person and to ensure that decision making for people who lack capacity is done appropriately and in accordance with the MCA.

RESEARCH AND THE MCA[32]

Research and consent is discussed in Chapter 14. The chapter that follows relates to research and the MCA.

There are clear rules about involving people in health and social care research studies when they are not able to consent to taking part. A family member or carer (the consultee) should be consulted about any proposed study. People who can be consultees include family members, carers, attorneys and deputies, as long as they are not paid to look after the person in question and their interest in the welfare of the person is not a professional one. If they say that the person who lacks capacity would not have wanted to take part, or to continue to take part, then this means that the research must not go ahead.

The research has to be approved by the relevant research ethics committee. A researcher must stop the research if at any time they think that one of the MCA section 31[33] requirements is not met (i.e. the research must relate to an impairing condition, have potential to benefit the person lacking capacity or be intended to provide knowledge about the same or a similar condition). This means that the researcher needs to understand the basis on which the research approval is given and ensure not only that the research is approved but that these requirements continue to be met throughout the period of the research. It is good practice for staff to ask to see evidence that the research has received approval.

If the person who lacks capacity appears to be unhappy with any of the activities involved in the research, then the research must stop.

Health professionals should note that there are separate rules for clinical trials.

PROTECTION[34]

Criminal offence under the MCA

Criminal offences of ill-treatment or wilful neglect.[35]

The MCA created a criminal offences of ill-treatment or wilful neglect, which may apply to the following:

➤ people who have the care of a person who lacks capacity
➤ an attorney acting under a Lasting Power of Attorney or Enduring Power of Attorney
➤ a deputy appointed by the Court.

Allegations of offences may be made to the police or the Office of the Public Guardian. They can also be dealt with under adult protection procedures (via adult services in social services departments). The penalty for these criminal offences may be a fine and/or a sentence of imprisonment for up to five years.

EXAMPLE

Mabel is 90 and has dementia. She lives with her son, Steven, who is her main carer and welfare attorney under a Lasting Power of Attorney. A community nurse regularly visits Mabel to assist with dressings. She is concerned that Mabel is always cold and hungry. She suspects that Steven is neglecting his mother.

The nurse alerts her manager and they contact the police and the local adult protection service. A police investigation is carried out and Steven is charged with the wilful neglect of his mother.

An IMCA is instructed to speak for Mabel, because her son, who would otherwise represent her, is possibly involved in the neglect.

In addition, the Court, in conjunction with the Public Guardian, also takes steps to terminate the Lasting Power of Attorney. Adult services (social services) are alerted and alternative care arrangements for Mabel are put in place.

The Public Guardian

The MCA creates a new public office – the Public Guardian – with a range of functions that contribute to the protection of people who lack capacity. These functions include:

➤ keeping a register of Lasting Powers of Attorney and Enduring Powers of Attorney
➤ monitoring attorneys
➤ receiving reports from attorneys and deputies
➤ keeping a register of orders appointing deputies
➤ supervising deputies appointed by the Court
➤ directing Court of Protection visitors
➤ providing reports to the Court
➤ dealing with enquiries and complaints about the way deputies or attorneys use their powers
➤ working closely with other agencies to prevent abuse.

Court of Protection visitors

These are individuals appointed by the Lord Chancellor who provide independent advice to the Court and the Public Guardian. They will have a role in the investigation of allegations of abuse of a person who lacks capacity. Their visits will include checks on the general well-being of a person who lacks capacity. They will also help and support attorneys and deputies.

Further information and guidance on their role and how to contact them will be provided by the Office of the Public Guardian as it becomes more established. These details are likely to be included in local adult protection policies and procedures.

MCA AND CHILDREN AND YOUNG PEOPLE[36]

Young people under the age of 16

The Mental Capacity Act (MCA) does not usually apply to children younger than 16 who do not have capacity. Generally, people with parental responsibility for such children can make decisions on their behalf under common law. However, the Court of Protection has powers to make decisions about the property and affairs of a person who is under 16 and lacks capacity within the meaning of the MCA if it is likely that the person will still lack capacity to make these types of decision when they are 18.

EXAMPLE

Jeremy was nine when he was in an accident and sustained severe head injuries causing permanent brain damage. He was awarded a significant amount of money in damages in the personal injury claim taken by his parents on his behalf. Jeremy is unlikely to recover sufficiently to have the capacity to be able to make financial decisions for himself when he reaches 18.

The Court of Protection makes an order appointing Jeremy's father as deputy to manage his financial affairs.

Young people aged 16 and 17

The MCA overlaps with provisions made under the Children Act 1989 in some areas. There are no absolute criteria for deciding which route to follow.

An example of where the MCA would be used would be when it is in the interests of the young person that a parent, or in some cases someone independent of the family, is appointed as a deputy to make financial or welfare decisions. This could apply when a young person has been awarded compensation and a solicitor is appointed as a property and affairs (financial) deputy to work with a care manager and/or family members to ensure that the award is suitably invested to provide for the young person's needs throughout their lifetime.

A 16 or 17-year-old who lacks capacity to consent can be treated under section 5 of the MCA. The person providing care or treatment must follow the MCA's principles and act in a way that they reasonably believe to be in the young person's best interests. Parents, others with parental responsibility, or anyone else involved in the care of the young person should be consulted unless the young person does not want this or this would otherwise breach their right to confidentiality. Any known views of the young person should also be taken into account. If legal proceedings are required to resolve disputes about the care, treatment or welfare of the young person aged 16 or 17 who lacks capacity, these may be dealt with under the Children Act 1989[37] or the MCA.

EXAMPLE

Katherine is 17 and has profound learning disabilities and lacks the capacity to decide where she should live. Her parents are divorcing and do not agree on where Katherine should live. In this case, it may be appropriate for the Court of Protection to deal with the disputed issue. This is because an order made in the Court of Protection could continue into Katherine's adulthood, whereas any orders made by the family court under the Children Act 1989 will expire on Katherine's 18th birthday.

Summary
➤ The MCA generally only applies to people aged 16 and over.
➤ The Court of Protection can be involved in decisions about someone under 16 if they are likely to continue to lack capacity to make those decisions when they reach 18.
➤ Only people of 18 and over can make Lasting Powers of Attorney and advance decisions under the MCA.
➤ A 16 or 17-year-old who lacks capacity can be treated under the MCA.

The MCA is different from the Mental Health Act 1983 (MHA). Some people may be affected by both Acts and this overlap.

Summary of the Acts

The MCA provides a framework for acting and making decisions on behalf of people of 16 years and over who lack the capacity to make decisions for themselves. The Act confirms in legislation the presumption that adults have full legal capacity to make their own decisions unless it is shown that they do not.

The MHA is primarily about people who are diagnosed as having a mental disorder that requires them to be detained and treated in the interests of their own health or safety, or with a view to protecting other people.

People who are detained under the MHA do not necessarily lack capacity to make decisions either about their mental healthcare or anything else. Even if they do lack capacity to make treatment decisions they may still have the capacity to manage their day-to-day affairs. They may be able to make decisions about their financial affairs and other matters. Their capacity to do this should be assessed in relation to the particular decision.

EXAMPLE 1

May is usually healthy and active. She lives alone and is in frequent contact with her family. However, a urinary tract infection causes short-term confusion. She is uncertain about where she is and does not recognise her daughter who visits her regularly. For a period of two weeks, she temporarily loses her capacity to make decisions, and while she is unwell her daughter manages her money for her, does the shopping and pays the bills. However, once she has been treated with antibiotics, her confusion clears and she is able to manage her own finances again.

May temporarily lost capacity to make decisions.

EXAMPLE 2

Bonnie is homeless. She sleeps in shelters and spends her time pushing a handcart around the city centre. She has an extreme fear of electricity and, as a result of this, has refused all offers of permanent accommodation. Bonnie develops a problem with her foot. Her community psychiatric nurse (CPN) arranges to take her to see a doctor who diagnoses gangrene in one of Bonnie's toes. She is referred to a hospital consultant who advises amputation of the infected leg from the knee down. Bonnie is adamant in her refusal to have the operation. Bonnie is able to explain that she understands the relevant information about her condition and the consequences of not having the operation to the consultant. She asks her CPN to be with her while she talks to the consultant and refuses the amputation.

Bonnie's capacity to make a decision varies according to the decision to be made.

EXAMPLE

Although Bonnie has a paranoid fear of electricity that makes it impossible for her to live permanently indoors, she is able to carry on with her life in a manner that suits her. She is perfectly able to make rational decisions about issues other than those related to her fear of electricity. It is important that Bonnie's decisions are respected. The amputation would make it impossible for Bonnie to walk around the city centre; this was very important to her and for her chosen lifestyle. She would have to be housed, probably in sheltered accommodation of some kind that would have electricity. It is unlikely that she would have stayed there long and would try to avoid services. This would cause a serious decline in her mental health and seriously impact on the quality of her life. It appeared that the consultant assumed that because Bonnie has a mental health problem, she lacked capacity in all areas of her life. Bonnie should be able to walk around the city centre, even though her foot will be painful.

The MCA specifies that a person is not to be treated as unable to make a decision merely because they make an unwise decision. The MCA reinforces the right to autonomy and the fact that each one of us is an individual with our own values, beliefs, preferences and attitude to risk, which may not be the same as other people's. Even if a person makes a decision which others, including family, friends or staff, view as unwise, unusual or irrational, this does not necessarily mean that the person lacks capacity to make that decision. There may be cause for concern if an individual repeatedly makes unwise decisions, which could place them at a significant risk of harm or serious exploitation. Concern may also be triggered if a person makes a particular decision, which defies all notions of rationality or is markedly out of character.

TASK

Bonnie's capacity to make her own decision was respected, even though it might be viewed as unwise as the gangrene in her toe would be likely to spread to her other toes and leg. Bonnie's ability to make this decision was not affected by her mental health problem.

How do you think you might have made a record of the decision-making process?

How do you think the CPN could best support Bonnie and communicate with her?

Using the Mental Capacity Act and the Mental Health Act to treat people who lack capacity to consent to treatment

The MCA can be used to treat people with mental health problems who lack capacity to consent. This applies to treatment for mental health problems, regardless of how serious they are, as well as physical health problems. The MCA cannot be used to detain people or deprive them of their liberty.

In some cases, both the MCA and the MHA will be options for those who are judged to need treatment, but the MCA can only be used for people who lack the capacity to make their own decision about treatment. The MCA will usually represent the less restrictive option. However, the MHA may need to be used when professionals judge the use of the MCA not possible or inadequate in the circumstances.

It might be necessary to consider using the MHA rather than the MCA if:

➤ it is not possible to give the person the care or treatment they need without carrying out an action that might deprive them of their liberty
➤ the person needs treatment that cannot be given under the MCA (for example, because the person has made a valid and applicable advance decision to refuse all or part of that treatment)
➤ the person may need to be restrained in a way that is not allowed under the MCA
➤ it is not possible to assess or treat the person safely or effectively

without treatment being compulsory (perhaps because the person is expected to regain capacity to consent, but might then refuse to give consent)

➤ the person lacks capacity to decide on some elements of the treatment but has capacity to refuse a vital part of it – and they have done so, or

➤ there is some other reason why the person might not get the treatment they need, and they or somebody else might suffer harm as a result.

EXAMPLE

Cindy has a bipolar disorder which is managed in the community by lithium treatment and ongoing support from a CPN. Her daughter is getting married in two months time and she is becoming increasingly agitated and ambitious in her planning for the event – she has already taken out large loans which she cannot afford and is up all night making lists and ringing hotels. Her psychiatrist suggests adding a major tranquilliser to her medication, but Cindy says that she needs to have lots of energy to plan the event and is concerned that the tranquilliser will slow her down. The psychiatrist consults the CPN and decides that Cindy currently lacks the capacity to consent to treatment but that he can administer a tranquilliser to her under the MCA without her consent. He considers that treating her now will be in her best interests as otherwise she is likely to miss or disrupt the wedding, which would be a huge disappointment for her and her family.

EXAMPLE

Keith, who has a history of psychotic episodes, is becoming increasingly anxious about the CCTV cameras in supermarkets which he feels are recording his every move. His CPN, is concerned that, although he appears to be managing other aspects of his life well, he has become embroiled in a number of angry arguments in his local village supermarket. Keith refuses to have his medication increased as he is unhappy about possible side-effects. His CPN is aware that Keith's history of violent behaviour means that he may pose a risk to others and arranges for him to be assessed for admission to a mental health unit under the MHA. The CPH considers that a short admission would allow for a full assessment and review of his medication.

The MCA allows Cindy, who is judged to lack capacity to consent to treatment, to be treated in the community without restriction of her liberty. In Keith's case, there are risks to other people if he continues to refuse treatment and he does not appear to lack capacity to consent to treatment. The MHA is therefore the appropriate means of delivering care and treatment.

The Mental Capacity Act and guardianship under the Mental Health Act

The MCA can be used to deliver care or treatment to service users in the community in circumstances where previously practitioners might have used powers of guardianship (MHA, section 7).[38] The MCA should be the first option considered. However, guardianship might be considered as an option in the following circumstances, where:

➤ decisions about where a person lives are placed in the hands of a single professional over a continuing period, for example when there have been long-running disputes about where the person should live

➤ the person is thought to be likely to respond well to the authority of a guardian

➤ explicit authority is needed to return the person to the place where they live; for example, someone is required to return to the hostel which they have left.

Using the Mental Capacity Act and the Mental Health Act in relation to inpatient admission, treatment and discharge

The interfaces between the Mental Capacity Act 2005 (MCA) and the Mental Health Act 1983 (MHA) are explained below.

Applications under the Mental Health Act

The principle that capacity is decision specific needs to be kept in mind when assessing people to decide whether an application should be made under the MHA. Even though formal admission under the MHA is being considered, people may have the capacity to make some decisions.

EXAMPLE

Mrs Kegan's family are very concerned about her welfare. She lives in sheltered accommodation, and has a long history of depression, but she now seems to believe that she still lives in her former family home. She is very distressed and keeps asking neighbours to take her home, and has recently taken an overdose of medication. The neighbours have contacted the GP because Mrs Kegan has now started to bang on their windows during the early hours of the morning asking for help.

An approved social worker (ASW) has assessed Mrs Kegan and feels, together with the GP, that a period of assessment in an inpatient specialist mental health unit is needed because Mrs Kegan is at risk (the overdose of medication is evidence of this) and appears to have a recurrence of her mental health problem. As she now lacks the capacity to consent to an admission and needs to be detained in order to be assessed and treated, the MHA and not the MCA needs to be used.

It is decided to admit Mrs Kegan to the inpatient unit for assessment under section 2 of the MHA. Although initially resigned to going to hospital, Mrs Kegan becomes very distressed about the care of her cats while she is away.

> A neighbour offers to look after the cats, as she has done on many previous occasions. Mrs Kegan gives her neighbour £50 to cover the cost of cat food. The ASW records in the notes that, although she is being admitted to hospital under the MHA, her decision to give her neighbour money is being made with capacity. In this case, based on what the ASW has witnessed, it is not necessary to consider taking any further action to help Mrs Kegan to manage her day-to-day financial decisions, just because she is being admitted to hospital under the MHA – although there will be some cases where that will be necessary.

Being admitted to hospital under the MHA does not mean that people have lost the capacity to make all (or even any) decisions.

Using the Mental Capacity Act as a less restrictive alternative to the Mental Health Act

The MCA can be used to admit people to in-patient care when they lack the capacity to consent to admission and admission is judged to be in their best interests, but it cannot be used to detain them in hospital. They should not be assumed to lack capacity to consent just because they refuse to be admitted to hospital.

Delivering day-to-day care to inpatients under the Mental Capacity Act

Best-interest decisions can be made to deliver day-to-day acts of care to in-patients who lack capacity to consent to particular acts.

Treatment for a physical condition

If an individual detained under the MHA needs treatment for a physical condition and there is a question about whether they have capacity to consent to it, their capacity should be assessed in accordance with the MCA. If they are found not to have capacity to make their own decision, then consideration should be given to what is in their best interests.

EXAMPLE

Elizabeth has been detained in hospital under the MHA for a number of years. She is diagnosed with breast cancer and advised to have a mastectomy followed by chemotherapy and radiotherapy treatment. She refuses both the mastectomy and the chemotherapy. Although Elizabeth is detained in order to receive care and treatment for her mental disorder, an assessment of capacity by her psychiatrist and a psychologist confirms that she is not lacking capacity to make decisions about her physical healthcare. She is able to explain to the oncology consultant that she knows the risks.

TASK

Consider how you would explain this to the ward staff if you were the medical practitioner involved in this case?

In other instances an individual will lack capacity to consent to or refuse treatment for a physical condition by reason of their specific mental disorder. Health professionals have a duty of care to consider taking a decision about physical health in the service user's best interests.

EXAMPLE

Miss Williams is currently in hospital receiving treatment under section 3 of the MHA. Miss Williams has a diagnosis of paranoid schizophrenia, and experiences delusions and hallucinations. She has a long history of treatment for mental health problems, but refuses all medical treatment, regarding it as unnecessary and part of a plot against her.

Miss Williams has recently developed an unusual swelling of her stomach. An ultrasound scan revealed suspected ovarian carcinoma (cancer). The

oncology consultant believes that a CT scan is essential for the proper investigation and treatment of the carcinoma and has informed her family of this, but
Miss Williams refuses to consent to a general anaesthetic or any further medical
procedures.

Miss Williams is assessed as lacking capacity to consent to or refuse treatment currently under the MCA's two-stage test of capacity, on the basis that
her mental illness causes an inability to understand the information regarding
the need for treatment or to use or weigh that information in order to reach a
decision.

The MHA is irrelevant here, but under section 5 of the MCA doctors are
able to provide treatment in the absence of consent, so long as the principles
of the MCA have been complied with and the treatment is in Miss Williams's
best interests.

The two cases of Miss Williams and Elizabeth are different. Miss Williams,
because of her specific mental health problems, lacks capacity in this
instance. This is because of the nature of her problems (such as her paranoid
feelings) and how they are shown in a thought disorder that is particularly
related to medical treatment. On the other hand, Elizabeth's specific mental
health problems have no impact on her capacity to make the decision about
the treatment options for breast cancer.

Consent to treatment for mental health problems

Both the MHA and the MCA require the person proposing to treat to establish an individual's capacity to consent to treatment. People with mental
health problems who are not detained under the MHA may be treated under
the MCA on the same basis as anyone else, if they lack capacity to make the
relevant decisions for themselves.

However, if a person is formally detained under the MHA, then, subject
to various safeguards, it may be possible to treat their mental disorder without
their consent (whether or not they have the capacity to give such consent). A
person detained under the MHA may be treated without consent but only for
the condition for which they have been detained. In many cases, treatment
for mental health problems can only be given without consent if a second
opinion appointed doctor (SOAD) has certified that it should be given, and
if the patient is refusing consent, or is unable to give it. The MCA does not
apply to treatment for a mental disorder given under Part 4 of the MHA.

Using the Mental Capacity Act in planning discharge from hospital

Regardless of whether or not a person is detained under the MHA, the individual's capacity to make decisions needs to be considered in planning for discharge from hospital or an assessment unit.

Anyone making a decision in the best interests of a person who lacks capacity is required by the MCA not to make assumptions that cannot be clearly justified. They are also required to involve the person in the decision-making process. They must encourage and enable their participation wherever possible.

Aftercare under supervision (Mental Health Act, section 25A)[39]

Where previously health professionals might have considered using supervised aftercare for a person being discharged from a mental health unit, the MCA might now be used to deliver care and treatment.

Health professionals should consider whether the MCA applies – but remember, the MCA can only be used when service users lack the capacity to make particular decisions.

Self-harm

Cases of self-harm present a particular difficulty for health professionals. Where the patient is able to communicate, an assessment of their mental capacity should be made as a matter of urgency. If the patient is judged not to be competent, they may be treated on the basis that they lack capacity in accordance with the MCA or under the MHA if appropriate.

Patients who have attempted suicide and are unconscious should be treated in an emergency as discussed below. If any doubt exists as to either their intentions or their capacity when they took the decision to attempt suicide.

Health professionals must remember that competent patients have the right to refuse life-sustaining treatment (other than treatment for mental disorder under the Mental Health Act 1983), both at the time it is offered and in the future. If a competent patient has harmed themselves and refuses treatment, a psychiatric assessment should be obtained. If the use of the Mental Health Act 1983 is not appropriate, then their refusal must be respected. Similarly, if practitioners have good reason to believe that a patient genuinely intended to end their life and was competent when they took that decision, and are satisfied that the Mental Health Act is not applicable, then treatment should not be forced upon the patient although clearly attempts should be made to encourage him or her to accept help.

CASE

In October 2009 a Coroner's Court ruled that Hospital staff acted within the law when they allowed a young woman to kill herself because she told them she wanted to die.

Kerrie Wooltorton, 26, suffered from depression. She had been treated at mental health units and had drunk lethal anti-freeze up to nine times in the preceding 12 months – but each time doctors had saved her. Miss Wooltorton wrote her living will on 15 September 2007, explaining that she was '100% aware of the consequences' of taking poison and that she did not want treatment.

Three days later she swallowed anti-freeze and called the emergency services before being taken to hospital where she told staff of her wishes and gave them the letter.

The advance directive stated that if she called for an ambulance it was not because she wanted life-saving treatment but because she did not want to die in her flat, alone or in pain.

Miss Wooltorton died in a hospital bed the following day but her family believe she should have been saved.

The coroner stated that 'She refused such treatment in full knowledge of the consequences and died as a result. . . . Any treatment . . . in the absence of her consent would have been unlawful'.[40]

THE MENTAL CAPACITY ACT 2005 AND THE MENTAL HEALTH ACT 1983 AND 2007

The Mental Health Act 2007 makes a number of amendments to the Mental Capacity Act 2005 and Mental Health Act 1983.

As previously discussed the changes to the MCA provide for procedures to authorise the deprivation of liberty of a person resident in a hospital or care home who lacks capacity to consent. The MCA principles of supporting a person to make a decision when possible, and acting at all times in the person's best interests and in the least restrictive manner, will apply to all decision-making in operating the procedures.

Documenting capacity issues

When documenting issues of capacity health professionals should ensure the detail is recorded very carefully. This should include the findings of the issue of capacity, how the patient's capacity was assessed and whether incapacity is permanent or likely to be long-standing, what is in the patient's best interests and why.

Documenting capacity is discussed in detail in Chapter 10.

Reports for the Court of Protection/Office of the Public Guardian

Formal reports or access to records may be required in certain circumstances by the Court of Protection or Office of the Public Guardian. It is therefore important that records are maintained and kept up to date.

Defence under the MCA[41]

When carrying out care and treatment in the best interests of a person who lacks capacity, health professionals will be legally protected. This means that where it has been established that the patient lacks capacity and has been treated without consent they will be protected from claims against them for treating without such consent provided they:

1 have taken reasonable steps to assess the person's capacity to consent to the act in question
2 reasonably believe that the person lacks the capacity to consent
3 reasonably believe that the act they are carrying out is in the person's best interests.

However, this does not provide a defence where the health professional has acted negligently.[42]

Further information on the Mental Capacity Act 2005 and how it applies can be obtained from the Department of Health.[43]

REFERENCES

1 Mental Capacity Act 2005
2 Mental Capacity Act 2005 Code of Practice
3 Mental Health Act 1983
4 Mental Health Act 2007
5 Statutory Instrument 2009 No. 1884. The Lasting Powers of Attorney, Enduring Powers of Attorney and Public Guardian (Amendment) Regulations 2009.
6 Mental Health Act 1983
7 Mental Capacity Act 2005, s 1; Code of Practice, c 2
8 Mental Capacity Act 2005, s 2; Code of Practice, c 4
9 Mental Capacity Act 2005, Code of Practice, 4.11–4.15
10 Mental Capacity Act 2005, Code of Practice, 3.10–3.16

11 Mental Capacity Act, Code of Practice, 4.44–4.49

12 Mental Capacity Act, Code of Practice, 5.1–5.69

13 Mental Capacity Act, Code of Practice, 5.13

14 Mental Capacity Act 2005, s 5

15 R (L) v Bournewood Community and Mental Health NHS Trust [1997] EWCA Civ 2879

16 European Convention on Human Rights, art 5

17 Mental Health Act 2007

18 Mental Capacity Act, ss 5 and 6; Code of Practice, 6.11–6.19

19 Mental Capacity Act 2005, s 5

20 Created under the Enduring Power of Attorney Act 1985

21 Mental Capacity Act, ss 9–14; Code of Practice, c 7

22 Mental Capacity Act, s 9

23 Mental Capacity Act, Sch 4; Code of Practice, c 7

24 Mental Capacity Act, Code of Practice, 5.63–5.64

25 Mental Capacity Act, Pt 2; Code of Practice, c 8

26 Mental Capacity Act, s 16(4)(a)

27 Mental Capacity Act, ss 24–27; Code of Practice, c 9

28 Mental Capacity Act, Code of Practice, 9.40

29 Mental Capacity Act, ss 35–41; Code of Practice, c 10

30 Mental Health Act 2007

31 NHS and Community Care Act 1990

32 Mental Capacity Act, ss 30–34; Code of Practice, c 11

33 Mental Capacity Act 2005, s 31

34 Mental Capacity Act, Code of Practice, c 14

35 Mental Capacity Act, s 44; Code of Practice, c 14

36 Mental Capacity Act, Code of Practice, c 12

37 Children Act 1989

38 Mental Health Act 1983, s 7

39 Mental Health Act 1983, s 25(a)

40 BBC News. Doctors 'forced' to allow suicide. Available at: http://news.bbc.co.uk/1/hi/england/norfolk/8284728.stm (accessed 15 March 2010).

41 Mental Capacity Act 2005, s 5

42 Department of Health. Available at: www.dh.gov.uk (accessed 27 July 2010).

43 Parts of the content of this chapter are reproduced under the terms of the Click-Use Licence.

CHAPTER 18

Advance decisions and advance statements

A patient may have an 'advance statement' or 'advance decision', sometimes referred to as a 'living will' or an 'advance directive', specifying how they would like to be treated in the event that they lose mental capacity in the future.

Such an advance statement or decision cannot be used by patients to:
➤ insist on the course of treatment or act against the professional judgment of the health professionals
➤ ask for their life to be ended
➤ nominate someone else to decide about treatment on their behalf.

An advance statement or decision cannot be ignored by health professionals. If treatment is given contrary to them the health professional may face civil liability or criminal prosecution.

Question

> What is the difference between an advance decision and an advance statement?

ADVANCE DECISION OR ADVANCE STATEMENT?

An advance decision is a decision to refuse treatment. An advance statement is any other decision about how a patient would like to be treated.

Only an advance decision is legally binding, but an advance statement should be taken into account when deciding what is in the patient's best interests.

An advance decision cannot be ignored by health professional. If treatment is given contrary to the advance decision the health professional may face civil liability or criminal prosecution.

Advance statement

This is a general statement of the patient's wishes and views. It states their preferences and what treatment or care they would like to receive should they, in the future, be unable to decide or communicate their wishes. It can include non-medical things such as food preferences and whether they would prefer a bath to a shower.

It may reflect their religious, cultural or other beliefs and any aspects of their life that they particularly value. An advance statement helps those involved in care to know more about what is important to the patient.

An advance statement must be considered by health professionals providing their treatment and care when they determine what is in their best interests, but health professionals are not legally bound to follow their wishes. An advance statement cannot be used by patients to insist on particular treatment if it is against the professional judgment of the health professional.

Advance statements can also be used to specify who health professionals should consult with when a decision has to be made, if the patient is unable to make that decision themselves.

A patient may create a Lasting Power of Attorney (LPA) to give someone else the power to make decisions about their care and treatment if they are not able to do so themselves. LPA is discussed in more detail in Chapter 17.

An advance decision to refuse treatment

An advance decision to refuse treatment is legally binding.

An adult with mental capacity can refuse treatment for any reason, even if this might lead to their death, as discussed ante. However, no one is able to insist that a particular medical treatment is given, if it conflicts with the health professionals' judgment.

An advance decision to refuse treatment enables an adult to make treatment decisions in the event of their losing their capacity at some time in the future. Such a decision properly made is as valid as a contemporaneous decision (made at the time) and so it must be followed, even if it would result in the person's death.

One of the difficulties often faced by health professionals is determining precisely in what circumstances an advance refusal applies. An advance decision to refuse treatment must indicate exactly what type of treatment the patient wishes to refuse and should give as much detail as necessary about the circumstances under which this refusal would apply. It is not necessary to use precise medical terms, as long as it is clear what treatment is to be refused in what circumstances.

EXAMPLE

David was suffering from motor neurone disease and was anxious to ensure that, as his disease progressed and he ceased to be mentally capacitated, he would not be given artificial hydration and nutrition (AHN). He therefore arranged to draw up a living will in which he made an advanced decision to refuse such treatment. The document was duly signed and witnessed. Only three months later he was severely injured in a road accident and brought into hospital unconscious. He was carrying his living will in his pocket and doctors were concerned that, if following an operation he required ventilation in intensive care, would the living will prevent them providing such treatment and care.

The wording of the advance decision is ambiguous. It states that he does not want AHN in the event that his disease progresses. The fact that he requires it as a result of a traffic accident is not within the ambit of the advance decision and therefore does not apply to this situation.

The Mental Capacity Act (MCA)[1] requires that advance decisions are made in a particular way. It is essential that health professionals involved in the care of a person who lacks capacity understand the difference between an advance decision to refuse treatment and other expressions of an individual's wishes and preferences.

Refusing life-sustaining treatment

If an advance decision involves refusing life-sustaining treatment, it has to be put in writing, signed and witnessed. If it does not involve life-sustaining treatment advance decisions can be verbal and do not need to be signed or witnessed if they are written down.

Even in the absence of an advance decision, people's views and wishes, whether written down or not, should be used to assist in planning appropriate care for the individual and making decisions in their best interests. Such statements of wishes and feelings are important, particularly if they are written down, but are not legally binding in the same way as advance decisions.

EXAMPLE

Mary, aged 74, is partially paralysed following a stroke and is treated in hospital following operations for a fracture. A nurse applies a vacuum dressing to the wound but Mary finds it painful and uncomfortable and asks the nurse not to use it again under any circumstances. This request is noted in Mary's notes. Mary is treated in hospital again a year later following another stroke when her operation scars are again a problem. On this admission, she is very confused and is not able to communicate clearly with staff. She is assessed as lacking capacity to consent to treatment. The doctor on duty suggests that a vacuum dressing be applied. However, the nurse notes from Mary's records that she has said in the past that she does not want this treatment ever again.

This is an advance decision that must be followed as Mary had capacity to make the advance decision at the time it was made.

When are advance decisions valid and applicable?[2]

An advance decision is valid when:

- ➤ it is made when the person who is over 18 years and has capacity
- ➤ the person making it has not withdrawn it
- ➤ the advance decision is not overridden by a later Lasting Power of Attorney
- ➤ that relates to the treatment specified in the advance decision
- ➤ the person has acted in a way that is consistent with the advance decision.

An advance decision is applicable when:

- ➤ the person who made it does not have the capacity to consent to or refuse the treatment in question
- ➤ it refers specifically to the treatment to be refused (it can do this in lay terms)

- the circumstances the refusal of treatment refers to are specified
- the circumstances the refusal of treatment refers to are present
- has not have been made under the influence or harassment of anyone else has not been modified verbally or in writing since it was made.

An advance decision to refuse life-sustaining treatment is applicable when:

- it is in writing (it can be written on the person's behalf by a family member, or recorded in medical notes by a doctor or on an electronic record)
- it is signed by the person making it (or on their behalf at their direction if they are unable to sign) in the presence of a witness who has also signed it – the witness is to confirm the signature not the content of the advance directive
- it is clearly stated, either in the advance decision or in a separate statement (which must be signed and witnessed), that the advance decision is to apply to the specified treatment, 'even if life is at risk'.

When might an advance decision not be followed?

An advance decision is not applicable if there are reasonable grounds for believing that circumstances now exist that the person did not anticipate at the time they made the advance decision and which would have affected their decision had they been able to anticipate them (e.g. new treatment), or if they have behaved in a way that raises doubts about or contradicts their advance decision.

A doctor might not act on an advance decision if:

- the person has done anything clearly inconsistent with the advance decision which affects its validity (for example, a change in religious faith)
- the current circumstances would not have been anticipated by the person and would have affected their decision (for example, a recent development in treatment that radically changes the outlook for their particular condition)
- it is not clear about what should happen
- the person has been treated under the Mental Health Act 1983 (when treatment could be given compulsorily under Part 4 of the Act. This applies to all advance decisions other than those that refuse

the administration of ECT, which cannot be overruled if valid and applicable).[3]

A doctor can also treat if there is doubt or a dispute about the validity of an advance decision and the case has been referred to the court.

A health professional may not override a valid and applicable advance direction on the grounds of the professional's personal conscientious objection to such a refusal.

An advance decision must be followed. If treatment is given contrary to the advance decision the health professional may face civil liability or criminal prosecution.

If there is doubt about the validity of an advance decision, a ruling should be sought from the court. Where life-sustaining treatment is refused in line with an advance direction, the patient should still be given basic care to make them comfortable until their death. This may include keeping the patient warm and clean and free from distressing symptoms such as breathlessness, vomiting, and severe pain. However, some patients may prefer to tolerate some discomfort if this means they remain more alert and able to respond to family and friends.

Health professionals must be able to recognise when an advance decision to refuse treatment is both valid and applicable.

A best interests decision to provide treatment cannot override a valid and applicable advance decision that refuses that treatment.

Protection from liability will not apply if a valid and applicable advance decision is ignored.

The decision of an attorney acting under a registered Lasting Power of Attorney will override an advance decision if the Lasting Power of Attorney has been made after the decision and gives the attorney the right to consent to or refuse the treatment specified.

There are special rules for people who are detained under the Mental Health Act 1983; in some circumstances, their refusal of treatment for a mental disorder may be overridden.

Advance decisions may not be valid if the individual made the decision while they had capacity and if they then did something that is clearly inconsistent with the advance decision.

EXAMPLE

Maria met with her solicitor to draw up her will and make arrangements for what she wanted to happen to her should she get an illness such as dementia. She had been shaken by what had happened to her sister during her last days in hospital and she wanted those caring for her to know that if she had a problem such as dementia, which meant that she lacked the capacity to consent to or refuse life-sustaining treatment, then she did not want to be resuscitated. She had tried to talk to her family about this but they found it morbid to talk about such things. She made an advance decision refusing resuscitation even if her life was at risk, which was written down, signed and witnessed by her neighbour. She told her family where it was kept, leaving copies with her GP and her solicitor.

Maria's wishes were respected and her family found it very helpful to have a clear idea of what she wanted. Healthcare professionals were required to follow her advance decision regardless of family members' views or wishes so there was no conflict when the question of resuscitation arose.

EXAMPLE

Sam made a signed and witnessed advance decision to refuse any treatment to keep him alive by artificial means. A few years later, he is injured in a rugby accident and is paralysed from the neck down and only able to breathe with artificial ventilation. Initially, he is conscious and able to agree to treatment. He participates in a rehabilitation programme. Some months later, he loses consciousness.

His advance decision is found although he had never mentioned it. His previous consent to treatment and participation in rehabilitation raise questions about the validity of the advance decision, as it is inconsistent with his actions prior to his lack of capacity.

So those making treatment decisions on his behalf decide that his recent actions in agreeing to treatment and participating in rehabilitation place doubt on the validity of his advance decision and continue to treat him.

Such decisions must be made on a case-by-case basis and must take all relevant evidence into account.

As part of empowering service users, health professionals need to develop means of promoting, implementing and recording this form of advance planning. NHS Trusts and user groups should develop guidance on the use of advance decisions and expressions of wishes.

REFERENCES

1 Mental Capacity Act, ss 24–27; Code of Practice, c 9
2 Mental Capacity Act, Code of Practice, 9.40
3 Mental Health Act 1983, Code of Practice 2008, 24.21

CHAPTER 19

Custody: consent for therapeutic and forensic intervention

The same basic principles of consent apply to people in custody. Those dealing with health intervention must have regard to and apply the law relating to consent as in any other health setting. Those involved in this area may include paramedics, nurses, GPs and police surgeons, among others.

Situations that may arise in a custodial setting will involve assessing the capacity of individuals to give their consent to examination and treatment. The individuals' capacity to consent may be affected by their being incapacitated, mental health conditions or the possibility that they are intimidated by their situation.

OBTAINING VALID CONSENT FOR HEALTHCARE INTERVENTIONS IN A CUSTODIAL SETTING

The same principles of consent that apply to patients also apply to those in a custodial setting. Consent must be obtained and must be given voluntarily, be informed, and so on, in order for consent to be valid.

Individuals must have capacity to consent. Capacity is discussed in details in an earlier chapter. The principles of capacity must be applied to a custodial setting. Remember they may have capacity to consent to some interventions but not others.

Lack of capacity to consent may be permanent, for example, through a mental health condition or learning difficulties. It may be temporary incapacity for example, through the use of drugs or alcohol, shock, fatigue or confusion.

Health professionals working in a custodial environment must be familiar with the rules of consent they must also be aware of additional issues that a detained person may give rise to. In a custodial setting, consideration must also be given to whether individuals are intimidated by their situation and not able to express their true feelings or beliefs.

CHAPTER 20

Cultural and religious beliefs

Some patients may refuse treatment or care because of their cultural or religious beliefs. For example, some patients may refuse medicinal products which contain animal products. Jehovah's Witnesses due to their religious convictions may prevent them from accepting blood or blood products, even when these are necessary to sustain life. In common with all patients the wishes of patients with religious beliefs should be respected throughout any care and treatment.

The health professional must not impose their own value judgments, either to give or not give treatment based on their own religious beliefs.

It is the responsibility of the health professional in charge of the patient's care to ensure that the position regarding the patients' wishes is clarified before the patient is admitted for the procedure in question. The responsible health professional should discuss with the patient the implications of any refusal to accept, medicine, treatment, blood or blood products. This should be at the earliest opportunity, and always before a decision is taken to recommend a procedure, which might, in normal circumstances, require the use of products or care they are refusing.

If a patient on a waiting list or scheduled treatment is discovered to be a Jehovah's Witness, then he should be contacted at the earliest opportunity to discuss the administration of blood and blood products.

If the patient's refusal of medicine, or blood and blood products is absolute, the health professional must decide whether he is able to treat the patient while fully complying with the patient's wishes. If he feels unable to comply with the wishes of the patient, then he should refer him or her to a colleague who does feel able to.

The health professional should be very thorough when providing information to the patients about the additional risks of refusing blood or medication. Occasionally, it will emerge during discussions, that the patient is willing to subordinate religious conviction to survival and allow the practitioner to use blood or blood products if this is necessary to save the patient's life. In these situations, it is essential to record the detail of this.

If a patient is unconscious and found to be carrying a card stating that as a Jehovah's Witness a transfusion must not be given in any circumstances, even if necessary to save life, the practitioner must respect the patient's wishes. Decisions should always be well documented.

Where the patient is a child, parents may not prohibit health professionals from administering necessary medication or blood or blood products to their children. However, consent should be obtained for the procedure, usually from the court where the parents refuse.

Where a parent refuses medication or transfusion of blood or blood products in the course of treatment of their child, practitioners must always seek legal advice. In emergency situations, practitioners may rely on the support of the courts to endorse decisions that are taken in good faith and in the best interests of the child concerned.

If the patient is under the age of 16 the health professional must assess whether the child is 'Gillick' competent. If he is and consents to treatment, the procedure should go ahead even if the parents object. Where time allows, legal advice should be sought. Consent and children is discussed in more detail in Chapter 11.

CHAPTER 21

Applications to court

In cases of serious doubt or dispute about an individual's mental capacity or best interests, an application can be made to the Court of Protection for a ruling. The duty officer of the Official Solicitor can advise on the appropriate procedure if necessary.[1]

The Mental Capacity Act 2005[2] established the Court of Protection to deal with decision-making for adults (and children in a few cases) who may lack the capacity to make specific decisions for themselves. The Court of Protection deals with serious decisions affecting personal welfare matters, including healthcare, which were previously dealt with by the High Court. In cases of serious dispute, where there is no other way of finding a solution or when the authority of the court is needed in order to make a particular decision or take a particular action, the court can be asked to make a decision.

The courts have identified certain circumstances when a referral should be made to them for a ruling of lawfulness before a procedure is undertaken. These are:

➤ decisions about the proposed withholding or withdrawal of ANH from patients in a permanent vegetative state cases involving organ, bone marrow or peripheral blood stem cell donation by an adult who lacks the capacity to consent

➤ cases involving the proposed non-therapeutic sterilisation of a person who lacks the capacity to consent to this (e.g. for contraceptive purposes), and

➤ all other cases where there is a doubt or dispute about whether a particular treatment will be in a person's best interests.

Other cases likely to be referred to the court include those involving ethical dilemmas in untested areas (such as innovative treatments for variant CJD),[3] or where there are otherwise irresolvable conflicts between healthcare staff, or between staff and family members.

The courts have stated that neither sterilisation which is incidental to the management of the detrimental effects of menstruation nor abortion need automatically be referred to court if there is no doubt that this is the most appropriate therapeutic response. However, these procedures can give rise to special concern about the best interests and rights of a person who lacks capacity. The need for such procedures occasionally arises in relation to women with a severe learning disability. It is good practice to involve as part of the decision-making process a consultant in the psychiatry of learning disability, the multidisciplinary team and the patient's family, and to document their involvement. Less invasive or reversible options should always be considered before permanent sterilisation. Where there is disagreement as to the patient's best interests, a reference to court may be appropriate.

It should be noted that, in the future, the courts may extend the list of procedures concerning which referral to the court is good practice.

Although some procedures may not require court approval, their appropriateness may give rise to concern. For example, some patients with a learning disability may exhibit challenging behaviour, such as biting or self-injury. If such behaviour is severe, interventions such as applying a temporary soft splint to the teeth or using arm splints to prevent self-injury are exceptionally considered, within a wider therapeutic context. As with hysterectomies undertaken for menstrual management purposes, great care must be taken in determining the best interests of such patients as distinct from dealing with the needs of carers and others who are concerned with the individual's treatment. The department of health has published guidance on referrals to court where capacity is in doubt.[4]

REFERRAL TO COURT AND CHILDREN

The general principles of consent and children are discussed in Chapter 11. The Mental Capacity Act (MCA) does not usually apply to children younger than 16 who do not have capacity. Those with parental responsibility for children under 16 years can make decisions on their behalf. The Court of Protection does have power to make decisions about the property and affairs of a person who is under 16 and lacks capacity within the meaning of the MCA if it is likely that the person will still lack capacity to make these types of decision when they are 18.

Where a child under the age of 16 lacks capacity to consent (i.e. is not Gillick competent), consent can be given on their behalf by any one person with parental responsibility or by the court. The child's welfare is acting in the child's best interests is paramount. The courts can overrule a refusal by a person with parental responsibility. It is recommended that certain important decisions, such as sterilisation for contraceptive purposes, should be referred to the courts for guidance, even if those with parental responsibility consent to the operation going ahead.

The European Court of Human Rights judgment in a case where doctors treated a child contrary to his mother's wishes, without a court order made it clear that the failure to refer such cases to the court is not only a breach of professional guidance but also potentially a breach of the European Convention on Human Rights. In situations where there is continuing disagreement or conflict between those with parental responsibility and doctors, and where the child is not competent to provide consent, the court should be involved to clarify whether a proposed treatment, or withholding of treatment, is in the child's best interests.[5]

Where consent is given by one person with parental responsibility it is valid, even if another person with parental responsibility withholds consent. However, the courts have stated that a 'small group of important decisions' should not be taken by one person with parental responsibility against the wishes of another, citing in particular non-therapeutic male circumcision and immunisation.[6,7] Where those with parental responsibility disagree as to whether these procedures are in the child's best interests, it is advisable to refer the decision to the courts. It is possible that major experimental treatment, where opinion is divided as to the benefits it may bring the child, might also fall into this category of important decisions.

REFERENCES

1 Further details about the Official Solicitor are available at: www.officialsolicitor.gov.uk/os/offsol.htm (accessed 27 July 2010). (Contact would usually be made through the legal department of the NHS body involved.)
2 Mental Capacity Act 2005, Pt 2 s 45
3 Simms v An NHS Trust [2002] EWHC 2734 (Fam)
4 Department of Health. *Reference Guide to Consent for Examination or Treatment.* 2nd ed.

London: Department of Health; August 2009. Available at: www.dh.gov.uk/prod_consum_dh/groups/dh_digitalassets/documents/digitalasset/dh_103653.pdf (accessed 18 January 2010).

5 Glass v The United Kingdom – 61827–00 [2004] ECHR 103
6 Prohibition of Female Circumcision Act 1985
7 Re J [2000] 1 FLR 571 at 577

Appendix: Consent algorithm

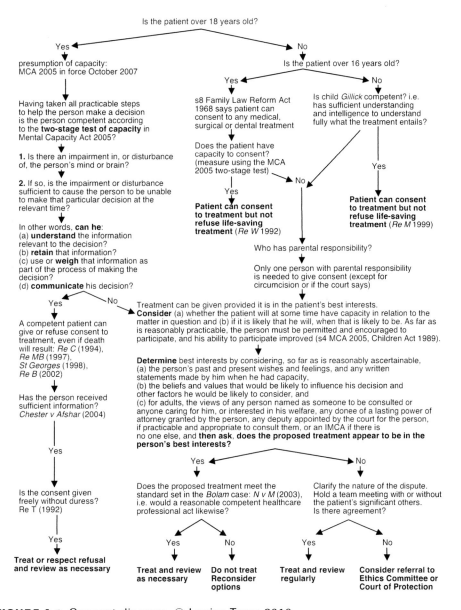

FIGURE A.1 Consent diagram. © Louise Terry, 2010

Glossary

Accountability	Someone who is accountable is completely responsible for what they do and must be able to give a satisfactory reason for it.
Act of Parliament	A document that sets out legal rules, a statute.
Advance decision	Allows an adult with capacity to set out a refusal of specified medical treatment in advance of the time when they might lack the capacity to refuse it if it is proposed. If life-sustaining treatment is being refused, the advance decision has to be in writing, signed and witnessed, and has to include a statement saying that it applies even if life is at risk.
Advance statement	A decision about how a patient would like to be treated, other than a refusal of life-sustaining treatment. An advance statement should be taken into account when deciding what is in the patient's best interests.
AHN	Artificial hydration and nutrition.
Assault and battery	Assault is an intentional or reckless act that causes someone to expect to be subjected to immediate physical harm. Battery is an intentional or negligence application of physical force.
Attorney	The person an individual chooses to manage their assets or make decisions under a Lasting Power of Attorney.
Balance of probability	Establishing the facts to the satisfaction of the court. The standard of proof in civil proceedings is on the balance of probabilities.

Best interests	The duty of decision-makers to have regard to a wide range of factors when reaching a decision or carrying out an act on behalf of a person who lacks capacity.
Bolam test	The test as to whether health professionals are in breach of their duty of care is whether a responsible body of medical practitioners would have acted in the same way.
Breach of duty	An act of breaking a law. Where there is a duty of care and that duty has not been met. Negligence is also referred to as a breach of the duty of care.
Capacity	The ability to make a decision.
Cauda equine	The nerves at the base of the spine. Cauda equina syndrome is caused by the compression of lumbosacral nerve roots and results in neuromuscular, urinary and bowel symptoms. It is a medical emergency and immediate referral for investigation and treatment is required to prevent permanent neurological damage.
Cavernous sinus pathology	The cavernous sinus is a large channel of venous blood creating a 'sinus' cavity bordered by the sphenoid bone and the temporal bone of the skull. It contains nerves including the cranial nerve, optical nerve and maxillary nerve. A cavernous sinus thrombosis is a blood clot within the cavernous sinus. This clot causes the cavernous sinus syndrome. Cavernous sinus syndrome is characterised by swelling of the eyelids and the conjunctivae of the eyes and paralysis of the cranial nerves which course through the cavernous sinus.
Civil law	The legal system which relates to personal matters, such as marriage and property, rather than criminal matters.
Claimant	A person who brings a claim, sues, for something which they believe they have a right to.
Common law	The legal system developed over a period of time

	from old customs and court decisions, rather than laws made in Parliament.
Compensation	Monetary payment to compensate for loss or damage. Also referred to as damages.
Contemporaneous	Happening or existing at the same period of time.
Criminal law	The legal system which relates to punishing people who break the law.
Coroner	A person appointed to hold an inquiry (inquest) into a death that occurred in unexpected or unusual circumstances.
Counsel	Another name for a barrister.
Court of Protection	Where there is a dispute or challenge to a decision under the Mental Capacity Act, this court decides on such matters as whether a person has capacity in relation to a particular decision, whether a proposed act would be lawful, and the meaning or effect of a Lasting Power of Attorney or Enduring Power of Attorney.
Court-appointed deputy	An individual or trust corporation appointed by the Court of Protection to make best interests decisions on behalf of an adult who lacks capacity to make particular decisions.
Damages	Monetary payment to compensate for loss or damage. Also referred to as compensation.
Decision-maker	Someone working in health or social care or a family member or unpaid carer who decides whether to provide care or treatment for someone who cannot consent; or an attorney or deputy who has the legal authority to make best interests decisions on behalf of someone who lacks the capacity to do so.
Declaration	A ruling by the court setting out the legal situation.
Defendant	A person in a law case who is accused of having done something unlawful.
Disclosure	Documents made available to another party or the court.

Donor	The person who makes a Lasting Power of Attorney to appoint a person to manage their assets or to make personal welfare decisions; or a person who donates tissue or organs.
Duty of care	The legal obligation.
Enduring power of attorney (EPA)	A power of attorney to deal with property and financial affairs established by the MCA. No new EPAs can be made after the Mental Capacity Act 2005 is implemented, but existing EPAs continue to be valid.
Fraser guidelines	Guidelines laid down by Lord Fraser in the House of Lords' case of Gillick regarding consent and children under 16 years. Referred to as Gillick competence.
GDC	General Dental Council is the professional body for dentists.
Gillick competence	A legal case which sets down guidelines to decide whether a child (16 years or younger) is able to consent to his or her own medical treatment, without the need for parental permission or knowledge.
GMC	General Medical Council is the professional body for doctors.
HPC	Health Professions Council is the professional body for allied health professionals.
Inquest	A court process to discover the cause of someone's death.
Independent mental capacity advocate (IMCA)	An advocate who has to be instructed when a person who lacks capacity to make specific decisions has no one else who can speak for them. They do not make decisions for people who lack capacity, but support and represent them and ensure that major decisions regarding people who lack capacity are made appropriately and in accordance with the Mental Capacity Act.
Lasting Power of Attorney	A power under the Mental Capacity Act that allows an individual to appoint another person to

	act on their behalf in relation to certain decisions regarding their financial, welfare and healthcare matters.
Law reports	Reports of cases decided by the courts.
Lawyer	A person who practises or studies law, such as a solicitor or a barrister.
Liability	Responsible for the wrong-doing or harm in civil proceedings.
Litigation	The process of taking a case to a law court so that an official decision can be made.
Negligence	Failure to do something or doing something that a reasonable person would not do. Breach of the duty of care is also referred to as negligence.
NHSLA	National Health Service Litigation Authority.
NICE	National Institute of Clinical Excellence (NICE) is an independent organisation responsible for providing national guidance on promoting good health and preventing and treating ill health.
NMC	Nursing and Midwifery Council (NMC) is the professional body for nurses and midwives.
No win, no fee	An agreement where legal costs will not be recovered by a solicitor if a claim for compensation is unsuccessful.
Parental responsibility	Assuming all the rights, duties, powers, responsibilities and authority that a parent of a child has by law.
Public Guardian	This official body registers Lasting Powers of Attorney and court appointed deputies and investigates complaints about how an attorney under a Lasting Power of Attorney or a deputy is exercising their powers.
Solicitor	A lawyer qualified to manage legal cases, give legal advice to clients, and represent clients in lower courts.
Standard of proof	Establishing the facts to the satisfaction of the court. The standard of proof in criminal proceedings is beyond reasonable doubt. The

	standard of proof in civil proceedings is on the balance of probabilities.
Statute	Act of parliament.
Strict liability	Liability for the criminal act where the mental element does not have to be proved.
Sue	Take legal action against a person or organisation by making a legal claim for money because of some harm that they have caused.
Tort	A wrongful act or omission for which compensation can be claimed.
Trespass	A wrongful direct interference with another person or with their property.
Vicarious liability	Legal liability imposed on one person or organisation for the torts or crimes of another, usually an employer is vicariously liable for its employees.
Witness	A person who gives evidence of what they saw, did or heard.

Index